THE NUCLEAR EFFECT

THE
NUCLEAR
EFFECT

The 6 Pillars of Building
a 7+ Figure Online Business

SCOTT OLDFORD

LIONCREST
PUBLISHING

THE NUCLEAR EFFECT

The 6 Pillars of Building a 7+ Figure Online Business

ISBN   978-1-5445-0705-7 *Hardcover*

978-1-5445-0704-0 *Paperback*

978-1-5445-0703-3 *Ebook*

978-1-5445-0731-6 *Audiobook*

For all the Entrepreneurs who are pursuing the path of their destiny,
for I wish you a path of momentum, success and fulfillment.

CONTENTS

INTRODUCTION

You are probably reading this book for the same reasons why I wrote it. And that is because of a powerful, innate desire to turn your vision into reality, to experience greater freedom in life, and because you *really* want to figure out how the heck to make this whole online business thing more successful. (With "success" here meaning *your* definition(s) and measure(s) of the word.)

In my twenty-plus years as an entrepreneur, The Nuclear Effect is the most powerful amplifier of success, freedom, abundance, and impact I have ever seen. It has reliably grown so many businesses that have learned and implemented it that I've lost count, and because of that, I deeply believe sharing it with more entrepreneurs through writing this book will satisfy that innate desire for me (and will help you satisfy yours if you make a serious commitment to making the concepts taught here work for your business).

And while businesses have been growing by activating The Nuclear Effect for a *long* time, it wasn't until 2017 that I truly began to understand and articulate exactly what was happening. As my understanding of this business phenomenon grew, I became better at guiding other entrepreneurs to be able to unleash The Nuclear Effect in their businesses as well.

The Nuclear Effect got its name because its impact on a business is similar to that of one of the most powerful forces known to mankind: the nuclear chain reaction. A nuclear chain reaction is when the initial nuclear reaction produces particles called neutrons. When these particles then harness some of the initial reaction's energy to set off their own subsequent nuclear reactions, the possibility for a (potentially endless) series of self-sustaining reactions is created. This nuclear chain reaction ultimately is responsible for exponentially increasing the amount of energy created and released from the initial effort. In fact, a nuclear chain reaction releases several million times more energy than *any* chemical reaction in history.

When The Nuclear Effect is harnessed by a business, six pillars arise to support it:

- Your Marketing creates a consistent, predictable flow of qualified leads for your business (without *you* personally needing to hustle to generate them). Leveraged, and often automated, generation of *quality* leads is the first element needed to unleash The Nuclear Effect.
- Your Sales become much easier to successfully close. The Nuclear Effect helps cement premium positioning in the market and bestows significant authority to your brand in the eyes of your potential clients.
- Your Product offerings become integrated and aligned in a way that allows for you to continue serving clients for longer periods of time and at higher levels of value.
- Your Operations become smoother, more efficient, and your business becomes more able to successfully run itself.
- Your Finances become more predictable and allow you to make sound planning and investment decisions (instead of always having to make financial decisions based on the realities of your short-term cash flow).
- Your Mindset becomes your greatest asset. Your ability to maintain composure and to make effective decisions during stressful times and high-pressure situations (and there will be plenty of both) is *the* thing that separates people who can only earn temporary success versus those who can truly sustain their success throughout their entrepreneurial career.

The bulk of this book will dive into each of these Six Pillars of business individually to show how to optimize each of them within your company. By the end, you will have the total blueprint for upgrading the operating system your business runs on, allowing you more profit and a more effective business.

When I first discovered that every part of a business can be defined by the Six Pillars, it blew my mind. Since then, I've shared this concept with hundreds of thousands of entrepreneurs, and time and time again, when it's used inside of a business, it has a powerful effect.

As you go through each Pillar, it will become clear how intimately all six are reliant upon one another and how *only* when all of them are truly working together and serving to strengthen the whole does The Nuclear Effect fully get activated.

This book is my mind's download after helping build dozens upon dozens of multiple seven-figure businesses that are oriented around creating profit, value, and impact in the market while allowing an entrepreneur to not lose their mind or sanity and giving them the ability to do what they love the most: create.

Truly, I *wish* someone had given me this earlier in my entrepreneurial career, and although there is a certain grizzled pride in having earned a lot of this the hard way, now more than ever, I believe in the value of collapsing time and leveraging the experience of others to accelerate *your* growth.

And while this book can help, there is no Easy button in business. Your business has to successfully create, market, sell, and then deliver *real* value in greater frequency, magnitude, and scale if you want to grow.

I've spent over twenty years—since I was seven years old, selling eggs from my parents' acreage—with many failures and successes, figuring out what is inside of this book.

Activating The Nuclear Effect will equip you with the ability to thrive in all phases of your business, but it is going to take focus, grit, and a commitment to play the long game. My intention in writing this book is to share everything I know about what The Nuclear Effect is, how to activate it to power your business's growth, and how to sustain that success over time.

My hope is to make a meaningful contribution to the happiness and success you experience on your entrepreneurial journey. It can be trying, difficult, and oftentimes lonely to pursue this path, but we keep pursuing it. It's in our blood. We are here to do something significant. It just happens that having a profitable business is *our* best path to making good on the potential we have within us.

I believe my mission and purpose for being on this planet is to help evolve who we are: *Homo sapiens*. Today, that means solving the problems of the entrepreneur so that entrepreneurs can solve the problems of the world. I've found that the more entrepreneurs are able to live in abundance, the more entrepreneurs who are successful, and the more who can live to find their truest why and go after it, the better our world can be. As a collective on this planet, we need us, and it requires that people like you stop playing small.

I'm excited to contribute to you succeeding in an entirely new life. And I am excited to have that potential you have inside you to go nuclear and do something truly great, important, and valuable for yourself, others, and the world as a whole.

WILL THE NUCLEAR EFFECT WORK FOR YOU? (AKA IS THIS WORTH YOUR TIME?)

The Nuclear Effect is something I've seen (and helped facilitate in creating) in many different sorts of industries, niches, and business models.

The Six Pillars are overwhelmingly the same across different industries. And whether you're B2B or B2C, really, you're *always* operating H2H, meaning Human to Human.

A common Mindset trap is to believe that your business or your industry is wildly different and distinct from others. That belief is a trap because it closes you off from gaining insight or wisdom from anything outside of that predefined box your business exists in.

This book *can* serve as an operating manual for how to build a business that is scalable, sustainable, and ultimately sellable, but only if you're open to seeing how the lessons apply for your company.

The avatar I'm writing this book to is an entrepreneur who runs an online business that sells some form of coaching, consulting, training, information, expertise, and/or live events.

I've operated businesses in so many different types of industries, online and offline; however, I believe one of the largest markets is one that operates online and that betters the transformation and ability to level up the consciousness of human beings.

So while this book was written with this type of entrepreneur in mind, know that the core principles and actionable advice here apply universally to business and have been implemented in every niche, geographic region, and language on earth. No special snowflake syndrome here, friend.

WHY YOU SHOULD LISTEN TO THIS

One of my favorite quotes is from Todd Herman, who has become a significant mentor, client, and friend: "If you want something, go get it. If you want something faster, go get it with a great mentor."

Success is often mainly about getting clear on *exactly* what you want and then creating the environment that will produce those outcomes. And that means you need to be incredibly intentional about the kinds of advice, direction, and mentorship you open yourself up to.

When I was seven, my dad brought home laying hens. I thought this was silly; we would need more. We would sell neighbors to our neighbors. By nine, I had over 100 chickens, until I realized they couldn't lay golden eggs. Further, without great optimization, we could only make around $10,000 per year, way too much work for that.

By the time I was eleven, I was working in the online realm as a programmer, using community forums to connect with others.

By the time I was thirteen, I was working with people across the world and was getting paid hundreds of dollars per hour for the work I was doing. Further, I was employing people across the world because I was a terrible programmer and was much better at marketing what I did.

By the time I was sixteen, I had my first office and my first mentor, and overnight, I went from an obese kid no one wanted to talk to and made fun of to winning a ton of awards and recognition in my small province of Newfoundland in Canada.

By the time I was nineteen, I expanded my businesses, had investments in various niches—including fitness, health, Software-As-A-Service—and was fully invested in a new type of technology for automobiles. Further, I helped others market their services, businesses, and everything in between. At one point, I had a physical office with almost twenty people.

By the time I was twenty-one, I was nearly $1,000,000 in debt. That happened quick, right? That's the fun thing about entrepreneurship, you can be up and then down, real quick. Maybe even faster than a casino—I'm up on roulette by $34,000 even though I only played three times.

When I was twenty-two, I sold my business for $1 and allowed them to take over my debt payments. On paper, I was acquired, but in reality, I just got myself a nice job. Further, I liquidated my other businesses and investments for pennies on the dollar.

Eleven months later, my business partner stole from me and had terrible business ethics (along with a terrible culture) and I decided that I wasn't going to peak at nineteen. I had less than $3,000 in my bank account and no available credit. I sold everything I owned and had three months of expenses in money, assuming I used my air-mile points for gas and groceries.

In 2013, I started a new agency. We did $1 million in sales within a year.

In 2014, I launched my first podcast and started my first entry into the entire online business world by building an audience. Further, around this time, I started talking about my story of debt (even if it wasn't paid off by a mile).

In 2015, I moved to Toronto, Canada, and launched my first online program, teaching online marketing—something I did since I was a kid. It was a MAJOR success even if my audience was less than 5,000 people online. In 2016, it generated millions of dollars—life started to go upward, I was able to pay off the debt I needed to—until I got an unexpected tax bill that was multiple six figures. In 2017, it did much better, and I was generating between $300,000 and $500,000 per month.

Now, there were a lot of things in between. A lot of trauma, a lot of really bad times, and a lot of really good times. But what happened next was the turning point.

See, there will come a time in every entrepreneur's life,

when they hit the self-actualization phase. This is where money is no longer a threat. This is where you can do almost anything. This is where you get to decide, "What do I want to do?"

See, I've always been REALLY good at being able to allow someone to see their best self. I've also been a really good marketer and exceptional at sales. Not because I'm good at lying or manipulation. Rather, I'm really good at understanding human beings.

I think it was all the books I read when I was a teenager. (I only learned how to read when I was eleven, so after that, I read A LOT.) But when it came to everything else? Operations, team, client delivery, finances. I SUCKED. I mean, I really, really, really, really was bad.

So I have this business; it's doing really well. But I don't feel fulfilled. And because the business didn't have all of the pillars set up correctly, I decided I didn't want to do it anymore. I wanted to take some time off. I wanted to travel the world. I wanted to explore myself. I wanted to go on the next great adventure. So, I let go of my team. I went nomadic.

And off I went. Only to meet my (now) wife three weeks later. The universe had other plans for me. And the plans it had were a lot less about doing less. And rather spending my time going inwards so I could externally create the success needed to fuel my mission, passion, and destiny in life, of helping humans evolve. All of this is still in the making.

However, today, living in Venice Beach, married to the girl I could only dream about when I was growing up. I'm able to invest, mentor, and advise various successful businesses and have a platform where I get to directly impact with what I teach to hundreds of thousands of people.

I'm far from the most successful person on the planet—and don't wish to possess that title, however, something that I realized about seven years ago. I have a unique way of seeing the world and synthesizing information so that someone like you is able to understand it in an easy way. I also feel like it's my obligation as I discover the easier way.

After building businesses, selling them, blowing them up, going a million dollars in debt, being hundreds of thousands in tax debt, being sued, all while making tens of millions of dollars before I was twenty-nine, I've got more than enough experience to help you to get to a point of living your best life.

A life where you don't have to work more than twenty hours a week. A life where you can travel the world whenever you want. A life where you can do really cool things that really light you up. A life where you have all your needs (and wants) met so you can accomplish your purpose on the planet. A life where you can do what you want, when you want, because you want to.

As you go through this book, I'm certain you'll see concepts, methods, and ideas that have been passed down from mentors of mine. I don't claim to know a lot. Rather, it's my ability to be a scientist, experiment with different concepts, and then tell others which ones worked (or didn't). The best artists steal (and still credit).

Let's dive in.

CHAPTER 1

STARTING IN A WEIRD PLACE

If you're reading this book and you're generating over $10,000 per month in revenue, you can skip this part. If you're generating under $10,000, here's what I can tell you. The Relevancy of this book is mixed. I don't want to guide you down a false road.

I say that because this book takes you through a process for upgrading every major Pillar of your business, but when you're under $10,000 per month, the absolute priority is upgrading your Marketing Pillar and your Sales Pillar. And usually this is an urgent, consistent source of pressure felt month after month just to keep the lights on.

If this is you right now, the thing you need more than anything is momentum. And while the Marketing and Sales sections of this book will definitely be valuable for you, the content of this book is largely built around what is going to create long-term, sustainable success.

But I wanted to include a special section specifically for those who need to generate an inflow of cash quickly—for those who need to create the breathing room necessary to truly begin building a long-term strategy for their business (as opposed to being continuously stuck in a short-term scarcity loop).

These are the *exact* steps I took to generate the cash I needed to begin pulling myself out of significant debt (I was $1,000,000 in debt by the time I was twenty-one years old) and to give myself the ability to invest in the right team, tools, and mentorship that has brought me to where I am today.

I reached out to every even remotely viable contact I had in email, LinkedIn, and Facebook with the intention of setting up a meeting with them.

Honestly, at the time, I didn't care who they were. I knew about the network effect and that even if that person wasn't someone that I could serve, they almost certainly knew at least one person that would be a good fit.

In total, over 200 meetings were set. I would do whatever worked for the other person. Lunch or coffee or Skype or a phone call. Whatever it took to get into a direct conversation with people, I was down for.

Once we were in conversation, I followed a simple five-step process:

1. I asked them about where they were and where they wanted to go.
2. I would help them clarify and understand the gap between the two better.
3. I showed them the possibility of a better future.
4. I showed them how I could help make that possibility a reality.
5. I told them about my situation at the time and why I was motivated to help them.

People hired me for anywhere from one-month- to twelve-month-long contracts. The total contracts' value was around $250,000 within sixty days. **I built a lean team of contractors and fulfilled on what I promised.** That was how I began to slowly climb out of the significant debt that had been built.

But back in 2012–2013 when that happened, I was essentially starting over completely from scratch, and I was *very* far behind the eight ball, so to speak. The mantra that spread among my team of contractors was, "We get shit done." And getting shit done consumed *my* life.

I worked eighteen hours each day for *months* to fulfill on *my* promises as well as to best position myself to being able to continue reducing the debt, but working that much is unsustainable. I don't recommend this path to *anyone*, save for maybe people who are in a similar situation as I was in and need to generate a *lot* of cash quickly, even if it means paying for it with all of your time and energy for a bit afterward.

However, don't forget: business is simple. Do what others aren't willing to do if you want to change your situation.

Here's the thing: the much more sustainable thing to do is build a profitable *business* that offers a valuable product that can be successfully delivered *without NEEDING* you to be the one who has to run, manage, or operate your business (including being the person who *has* to deliver and fulfill on the business's promise to your paying clients).

So if you don't have a *validated* product yet, the Product Pillar chapter is going to change the game for you.

Once you're clear on exactly **who** you want to serve, and you're clear on exactly **what** you want to offer them (aka your product), but you are regularly having months with collected revenues under $10,000, here is what I recommend you do to break that barrier (and start building some real momentum):

1. Forget about a funnel or going one to many right now. Your job is to create connections and make offers. As you'll see later in this book, Intimacy is *the* thing that gets money to exchange hands. Which brings us to number two: what you must do to make the right connections and make Relevant offers to them.

2. Find exactly who you believe you can serve best, the people who would benefit most from your unique, unfair advantage. Your path right now is to prove that you can get a consistent flow of people to trust that you can deliver the results they want and to choose to do business with you.

3. Start building a strong network (and an even stronger inner tribe). Host group lunches with people who are local to you. Build a Facebook group that anyone in the world can join and contribute to. Even if you're relatively early on in your journey of building expertise and achieving mastery, you can *always* be a connector for other people and always be looking to add value.

4. Commit to creating content. I've found that the more consistent you are, the better your content gets. And even if you need to exhibit a bit of courage, share it consistently too. Even if no one is listening right now, it's okay. Challenge yourself to write at least 1,000 words

per day and/or record one video per day. You want to build the habit of being more of a producer than you are a consumer. And besides, you need to get good anyways.

5. Stop boxing yourself in to what you *think* you *have* to sell or offer in order to generate revenue. Meaning that if you can help solve a problem or fill a gap for someone, but it isn't the thing you want to sell, I encourage you to consider making custom offers to people while you're looking to start really getting off the ground. It might be a little bit painful and less efficient, but the money will give you momentum, and then the momentum can give you *a lot* more money made in a much more painless way.

6. Hire someone as SOON as you can. Most entrepreneurs early in their business won't pull the trigger on hiring until things are really starting to hurt. The thing is, no matter how much you think you're #hustling every day like Rick Ross, humans typically max out at about eight hours of productivity per day. And sure, you can really go for it for a while (like I did a few years ago), but it *will* catch up with you sooner or later. You need sleep and relaxation and a whole lot of other things in life if you're going to be able to bring your best self to work each day. Anything less is simply robbing your business, your clients, and yourself of what *could* be if you chose to take care of yourself better, not to mention, you deserve it. There is nothing as powerful as adding more minds, perspectives, time, and energy that gets

invested into your business by a collective team. Growing the team at 1MT has been one of the greatest joys of my life and has only inspired me to take even better care of myself (so that I can show up that much more powerfully for the team, our clients, and everyone who follows my content).

7. Be intentional about the relationships you want to build and deepen. Find out what is Relevant to them and engage them on it. Support them on their mission and toward their goals. Do easy extra steps, like sending them something physical in the mail or using the network you're building from #3 to make potentially valuable introductions for them.

8. Take a deep breath and remember this perspective: you are in the top 97 percent of wealth in the world, and relatively speaking, your problems aren't *that* big. People far less intelligent, capable, and gritty than you have achieved the kinds of things that you are aiming at. Stay focused, stay positive, and follow solid advice. (Your gut usually knows what is worth pursuing and what isn't.) You'll get there. Hopefully, I can help you get there faster.

9. Find three to five people who are in the same place as you are in business, find three to five people who are a step or two *ahead* of where you are now, and find three to five people who are a step or two *behind* where you are now. To really move forward fast, it is powerful to have this unique combination of perspectives available

to you. Here, you have successful examples to follow, a crew of comrades supporting each other as you face similar challenges, and you have a couple people who you can support or mentor a bit to help them grow. There is a hidden benefit to that last part. Teaching something to others will help solidify your mastery of the subject and will hold you to a higher standard to live in consistent alignment with the good advice you give to others. When you have all three of these positive influences, you almost inevitably start accelerating your growth.

10. Stop following so many people. This goes back to producing more and consuming less. You'll have better results going *deeper* in listening to a small handful of people who you *know* can help light the way toward the goal(s) you want to achieve. Consciously choose a couple people who you believe are *best-suited* to help you reach your *current* goals and commit to implementing what you learn. Have high standards and have a dutiful attitude toward executing the strategy you decide upon. All other content is just noise. Every other business activity is just a distraction.

11. Focus on the next ninety days and forget everything else. Your purpose for now is to create enough momentum to begin taking long-term views and planning to *make your impact*. Don't go for the moonshot now. For the time being, go for what can create momentum and money.

12. Go the extra mile. Most people don't (which is why it

stands out so much). Make that your default intention behind anything you do for your audience, your prospects, and your clients.

13. Focus on playing your game and giving your best each day. Most of what you see online are lies, so don't fall into the vicious trap of comparison because *that* game is completely rigged against you.

14. Seriously, you don't need a marketing funnel right now. Nail down being Relevant to the *right* people. By the time you *know* that you're able to reliably get the *right* people to understand who you are, what you do, and agree to pay you to do it for them, then you know creating your funnel and becoming omnipresent to a bunch of the *right* people is going to bring you serious results and momentum.

15. Be diligent about delegating. Figure out the lowest value things you do regularly and give them to an employee or a VA or to a low-cost system of some sort. You want to be lean with cash, but you *need* to use a lot of discretion when it comes to your time and your energy. Create a regular habit of freeing up bits of time and energy for yourself and commit to reinvesting it into the *highest value* things that you can do. This one practice will change your life.

If you're not yet consistently clearing the $10,000 per month revenue mark, focus all of your energy in execution on the steps above.

And when you're not out there building momentum, the rest of this book can help you get a clear vision of where you want to ultimately drive your business toward. There definitely are some major growth headaches you can save yourself from when you build your business with intention from the ground up. I want to leave you with one little piece of advice.

If you're generating less than $10,000 per month, know that the ability to have a multimillion-dollar business shortly is completely possible. I've seen it time and time again.

In this book, I share the Six Pillars. The more you know these pillars, the better choices you can make. Having a successful business and being a successful entrepreneur is mostly about making good choices over and over in succession. The more you say yes and no to the right things, the faster you gain the momentum to have a successful business.

Let's introduce you to the foundation: the major Six Pillars that your business is built on.

To access the resources for this chapter, visit: www.thenucleareffect.com/resources/.

CHAPTER 2

THE SIX PILLARS OF A MULTIMILLION-DOLLAR BUSINESS

If you are going to grow your business, it is important that you expand out from a stable base and foundation. There are way too many unknown risks and unforeseen potential pitfalls in the game of business to gamble on growth before you're ready for it. In fact, if you don't have the proper foundation, then growth is only going to make your existing problems *even worse*.

If you scale a business without the right foundation, you're going to scale a broken system, which will always, at some point fail. You'll either run out of time, money, or have so many customer problems that new customers won't want to work with you. There will be more fires to put out, more extreme feast and famine cycles, and you'll be hustling harder because *you need to create even more cash each month* to keep your growing business operating.

Essentially, if you currently have a company that more resembles a hamster wheel than it does a real business, then the main thing that happens when you grow that company is that you're simply going to end up with a bigger, more exhausting hamster wheel (that also *carries much more risk* due to the higher stakes).

If you scale a loss, you'll only lose more. And that means, sometimes, you'll need to pivot, pivot, and pivot until you lock it in.

It is honestly *never* too early in a business to get a *clear picture* of how you want your business to be this time next year (or next quarter or what it needs to look like in order to be able to sell it). And no matter how big your business is or how much previous success you've enjoyed, there is *always another level* in this game—whether it's the next revenue goal or if it's upgrading your relationship to the business so that it better serves you and your life. There is *always* value in spending time to get clear on precisely where you want to get to.

If you are not clear and able to articulate *exactly* what you want, how do you expect to get *exactly* what you want most?

Set your target, decide that you will make it your reality, and then make it real through your commitment in action over time.

These chapters covering each of the Six Pillars are set up partially as a narrative for showing how these Pillars *can* work together so well that they set off The Nuclear Effect and partially as a playbook for things that you can implement into each of the different Pillars in your business. Even if you aren't quite ready for some of these plays, reading them can give you a clearer view into what you eventually may *want* these parts of your business to look like.

Similarly, if you are *already* doing some of these plays, reading them may show you some insight into some nuance or distinction or better articulation of *why* it works well so you can create better processes, better communication, and leading in demonstrating to your team that you can *always* be on the lookout for ways to potentially improve upon what you're already doing.

I believe that a business is just a set of systems, the Six Pillars are just the six systems that are present inside of your business. The more they truly act like systems, the easier it is to grow and scale and bring yourself further and further out of the business.

Build these systems into your business. Revisit them and upgrade them regularly. Get clear on where you want to go and move toward them with intent. Invest your energy to make your vision come alive as the Six Pillars begin powerfully working together and activating The Nuclear Effect in your business.

One of the best things you can do for your business is to take a deep, honest look at each of the Six Pillars in your business on a regular basis *and* log the results each time so you can look back on it over time. This will show you opportunities, risks, and patterns that need your attention if you want your business to thrive. It is a difficult exercise, but it is an incredibly powerful mirror that will show you paths to success.

We have a *free* tool for entrepreneurs where you can fill out a Six Pillars assessment as often as you would like to keep a running log and record of your business's growth and evolution. I recommend doing it monthly; however, if your business isn't stable, weekly is something I did for years. The thing is: you can't solve the problems you don't know about, and once you do, everything changes.

Further, bringing this and using it inside of your company

with your team members is a game changer. If you have your entire team sharing *their* biggest issues and challenges, and you solve those problems as a team, not only will it allow you to cover more ground, but it will allow you to be united.

Remember, you only have forty hours a week, at maximum. However, if you have a ten-person team, you have 400 hours a week. (It might also be interesting for you to fill out the assessment once now and then once again after reading the Pillar sections and implementing some things.) Bottom line: without actual implementation, all of this will remain merely theoretical.

While it's nice to learn stuff, it will die with you if you don't find a way to express, share, or create it in reality into your business. As mentioned in the opening introduction, if you want something, then go get it. And if you want something faster, go get it with a mentor who is familiar with the path that leads to the thing(s) you want.

The following chapters outline and detail some of the exact things I recommend when mentoring an entrepreneur to help improve in each of these Six Pillars. Whether you are looking to get off the hamster wheel, or you're in a place where you are ready to sustainably scale your business, I hope there is plenty in these chapters to help you clarify your vision and achieve your goals.

On the next few pages, you'll see a quick preview of what each Pillar chapter holds, and then we'll get you right into the Marketing Pillar to teach you about The Relevancy, Omnipresence and Intimacy Marketing & Sales Method—what I believe is the most powerful way to build a multimillion-dollar business.

To access the resources for this chapter, visit: www. thenucleareffect.com/resources/.

CHAPTER 3

THE SIX PILLARS EXPLAINED

PILLAR 1: MARKETING AND LEAD GENERATION

Successful marketing that consistently generates qualified leads is the lifeblood of your business. It's a massive part of what The Nuclear Effect is, and without it, you'll always come up short (while adding a lot of stress).

Unfortunately, many entrepreneurs choose hustling as their main marketing strategy. Either that or they rely on unpredictable lead sources, like organic social media, networking, referrals, or various outbound sales efforts. Or if you have some type of marketing that works, you rely on a single source of new potential business—that's a huge no-no.

Someday, it will go away. Relying on those is a surefire recipe for either burning out or for being forever trapped on the unpredictable revenue rollercoaster (or both). The *only* way off of that emotionally abusive ride is to install an automated, predictable, and scalable source of new quality leads.

In the Marketing Pillar, I will give you an in-depth look at The Relevancy, Omnipresence and Intimacy Marketing & Sales Method. This is the revolutionary marketing methodology that's been developing over my now twenty years as an entrepreneur. At this point, I've spent millions of dollars of my company's money as well as millions more of my client companies' money in ad spend to fully understand and perfect this powerful method.

The Relevancy, Omnipresence and Intimacy Marketing & Sales Method will show you how to consistently generate quality leads, build actual connections with them, and become the clear leader in your field, industry, or niche in their minds. (All of which combine to help them see *you* as *the* authority above your competition and have them happily pay premium prices to be able to work with *you*.) This is the method that is powering so many of the businesses that are growing rapidly and exponentially in the marketplace and are based on some of the best principles in marketing.

PILLAR 2: SALES

While it is great to be able to attract a growing stream of qualified leads to your business, you're ultimately wasting the fruits of your marketing efforts if you aren't able to powerfully (and consistently) enroll them into your product, service, program, or event. There is nothing worse than squandering the opportunity to solve a painful problem for someone (and getting paid well to do it).

In this section, I'm going to give you a lot of Mindset tips on Sales (because Sales is largely about your inner game) as well as the most powerful selling framework I've ever seen. This four-phase process for selling is simple, powerful, and *feels* good instead of awkward or stressful or icky (for both you *and* for the person you're on the sales call with).

I'll also show you how to use some of the amazing social connection and messaging tools we have available to us now to move sales conversations forward (and ultimately shorten your sales cycles) and be a LOT less salesy.

PILLAR 3: PRODUCT

In order to really thrive, your business needs a product that delivers a ton of value in a systematic way for your clients. That means your business is creating powerful results for people *without* relying so much on you to deliver those results.

Poor product design is one of the major reasons why talented entrepreneurs get stuck on the hamster wheel. By redesigning the things you offer to the market, you can create greater leverage for yourself (as well as greater profitability for your business).

In this Pillar section, I'll show you how to design products that support your business's long-term growth. After reading it, you'll have a clear picture of how to build an integrated suite of products that powerfully serve your clients and significantly increase your average lifetime customer value.

And by the end, you'll have a product you are proud to put your name on (even if *you* aren't personally involved in delivering *any* of it).

PILLAR 4: OPERATIONS AND TEAM

Solid operations are THE thing that will allow you to truly scale your business. Even if you had an endless line of people beating a path to your door trying to hurl their credit cards at you to buy your Product(s), your business would break from trying to take on more clients than its operational capacity could handle.

Lots of businesses die not of starvation, but rather, they die of the indigestion that follows reckless growth efforts.

The mild symptom of this is the feast-and-famine cycle in which you sell a whole bunch only to then realize your current team and operations aren't equipped to deal with supporting this many clients. And as a result, you're left scrambling to pick up the slack, put out fires, keep clients happy, rush your way through a fast hiring decision or two, and abandon your marketing and sales efforts in order to fulfill on your promise(s) to clients. After you're done serving those clients, you now need to get even more to pay for your newly expanded team, and you're at a disadvantage because you took your foot off the gas from a marketing and sales perspective. Unaddressed, this cycle gets more and more vicious until it eventually breaks the business (and/or the entrepreneur running it).

In the Operations Pillar, I'll show you how to hire the right people at the right time, how to build a culture of empowerment among your team, and how to always stay a step ahead in your operational capacity (so that you can experience more predictable growth).

PILLAR 5: FINANCES

Finance can be a pretty taboo subject for a lot of entrepreneurs. It can be tempting to stick your head in the sand instead of committing to staying on top of your numbers regularly.

Businesses die for three main reasons. They starve from

not making enough sales, or they die from indigestion from trying to grow too fast, or they die due to poor financial planning and management. As an entrepreneur, you don't need to have a CFO level understanding of Finance, but there are a small handful of key things to know that will help you consistently make intelligent financial decisions.

This Pillar is going to help you change your relationship to your business's finances as well as give you a couple of simple tools and frameworks you can utilize to make sound choices (especially during the times where you are feeling a lot of stress, fear, or scarcity in your business).

PILLAR 6: MINDSET

We entrepreneurs have a *powerful* ability to create. And the direction you have your thoughts, vision, and Mindset pointed toward inevitably shows up in the actions you take and *creates* the results, the business, and the life you are currently experiencing. Because of that, I am of the opinion that Mindset is truly the most important of the Six Pillars to building a thriving business.

The truth in life is that *no matter how successful you become, there is always another level.* And no matter how much you grow, there will *always* be thing(s) you struggle with.

In 2019, I sold a business of mine; however, before that, I

would spend time each week attempting to figure out how I could put my business out of business. At the time, I was helping over sixty, seven-plus-figure entrepreneurs all grow to the next stage, and one day, I realized my critical flaw with helping all of these entrepreneurs.

Entrepreneurship and the success of an entrepreneur, may come down to a lot of things, however, the biggest? Mindset. It's why, when I mentor and advise others, it's so much on Mindset. It's why I have investments and own companies that orient around the human mind. And with nearly every entrepreneur that I've helped, it's been 75 percent Mindset, 25 percent tactics. So, while this book will be super helpful for the tactical and strategic-driven type, it's more about having an open mind than even the right plan.

To access the resources for this chapter, visit: www. thenucleareffect.com/resources/.

CHAPTER 4

PILLAR #1: MARKETING AND LEAD GENERATION

Most people know me because of my marketing. People have introduced me as this guy knows marketing. I like to think of marketing as the ability to understand the human mind and meditate attention toward your signal, ensuring that the signal is understood and is actioned. Because that is marketing.

Your business is hungry, and if you haven't noticed, the main thing it eats is cash, and likely far more than you'd like. It needs money to keep operating month after month.

In order to survive, your Marketing needs to create just

enough new qualified leads, and in order to *truly thrive*, your Marketing needs to create an abundance of quality leads (and ideally generating them in an automated way).

Tell me if any of these sound like your Marketing efforts:

- You are caught on the Launch Loop (*needing* to do launches to generate enough revenue to keep the business running for the next stretch of months. Translation: you are possibly one bad launch away from being out of business).
- You have goals and projections for your Marketing efforts, but you have *no* idea how to reach them.
- Instead of being committed to a real strategy, you are using the spaghetti method (meaning you keep throwing a bunch of stuff at the wall and seeing what sticks). Plenty of businesses scale to multimillions with this still being the case.

On top of that, a lot of entrepreneurs who **do** generate a lot of quality leads gain them mostly through hustle. While there is a lot to be said for the hustler's skillset and the ability to attract and sell to people (it's certainly saved my ass several times), you're playing a dangerous game if you are *relying* on it to stay in business, and you're playing an impossible game if you're planning to scale a business by hustling harder. If *any* of this sounds familiar, you are firmly stuck on the entrepreneurial hamster wheel.

As you scale, you need to diversify your marketing. It must get better. As you scale a multimillion-dollar business, if you're reliant upon one type of lead or if your personal brand is generating all the business, you're in trouble.

While there are a handful of things that need to happen in all Six Pillars in your business to truly get off the hamster wheel, one of the first, and most important, steps to having a business that can run itself profitably is to create a predictable, scalable marketing system that generates an abundance of new leads (and effectively nurtures those leads) in an automated fashion. Experiencing this abundance is the initial spark that begins to set off The Nuclear Effect in your business and gives you an asset you're going to need if you want to grow: money.

Because of that, this Marketing Pillar section is going to show you each of the major elements that need to combine in order to ignite that spark:

- How to become the most Relevant person (or business) inside of your niche, allowing you to create powerful messages that resonate and direct massive attention from those who you serve.
- Why it's extremely important that messaging doesn't neglect 97 percent of your entire audience and how most entrepreneurs completely mess this up.
- The exact method to be able to leverage your brilliance,

expertise, and knowledge so that you can ensure the right person is able to see it at the right time and the right place.

- How to hack attention so that you can use some of the most powerful marketing (and human psychology methods) without having to be a grade A+ marketer or a prof in human psychology.
- Why it's important that you are small and aren't a massive business—the smaller the audience you have can be your biggest advantage.
- How to *leverage* the best content plus messages you create so they are seen by the right people (at the right time and in the right place).
- How to build greater connection with people so they want to buy from, partner with, or support *you* (over the other choices they have in your marketplace).
- And, well, a lot to help you if you've ever said:
  - My marketing sucks.
  - I need more leads.
  - I'm scared to run out of new customers.
  - I probably shouldn't rely on _____ for my business.

Remember, manifestation isn't a marketing strategy.

If you've been *stuck* on your own personal version of the hamster wheel and you've had enough of exhausting yourself running on it day after day (but not covering as much ground or experiencing as much growth as you would like in exchange for your efforts), allow me to introduce you to The Relevancy, Omnipresence and Intimacy Marketing & Sales Method, the most powerful way to turn strangers into customers, at scale, in the world.

THE RELEVANCY, OMNIPRESENCE AND INTIMACY MARKETING & SALES METHOD

At its core, The Relevancy, Omnipresence and Intimacy Marketing & Sales Method is about building profitable connections with people at scale. It's about making sure that the people who you *most want* to know who you are and what you have to offer not only see your messages but are compelled to consume and consider them. It's about treating people well and serving them with value before any money ever exchanges hands.

Further, it's about being able to distribute your brilliance and genius in the form of content to the right people, at the right place, while ensuring that it resonates, is Relevant, and has the attention required for those people to be attracted to you and turn that attention toward your signal so that eventually you'll be able to serve them at the highest level possible.

You see, entrepreneurs now have the most powerful marketing tools ever created available to them, and unfortunately, a lot of these tools get misused (if they get used at all). Because of how fast, instant, automated, and yes, even *fake* these modern marketing tools can be, a lot of entrepreneurs forget about some of the core principles of Marketing or rather, the principles about how to be human and to help humans.

These principles are the same as they've always been. What works in driving people to make their buying decisions progresses at the same pace as evolution. Winning people's attention, creating a connection, building trust, showing up consistently to be top of mind and making clear, valuable offers can't be replaced by an automated webinar or a fake countdown timer on a sales page or through brute-forcing uncompelling messages onto people through retargeting efforts.

Simply put, brute force, doesn't work, or at least, it's really expensive. Illumination of a problem, of a process, of a solution will always win instead of manipulation. When you are able to combine effective marketing principles with the full power of the tools now available, you ignite that spark that sets off The Nuclear Effect. That all starts here with The Relevancy, Omnipresence and Intimacy Marketing & Sales Method.

R.O.I. STANDS FOR RELEVANCE, OMNIPRESENCE, AND INTIMACY

Relevance refers to the quality of the messages you're

sending. It's how you win attention, it creates the way your business is positioned in the minds of others, and it determines how the offer(s) you make to the market are received.

It's what you are saying to your market that attracts people into your world. It's what compels them to invest with you to help them solve their problem(s) or deliver some desired result(s). It's what allows someone to say, "This is for me."

Omnipresence is the strategic distribution of your message, brand, and marketing. When your audience feels like everywhere they look, there you are.

And beyond being merely always present, they come to realize that they are always learning something valuable from you or seeing examples of the kinds of results you deliver or are feeling more and more connected to *you as a person*, basically, through your regular ability to share your messages with the people in your audience, you become incredibly Relevant to and intimate with them.

Omnipresence essentially is an *amplifier* of your Relevance and your Intimacy, building those two things in an automated, systematic fashion. When executed really well, you can be incredibly precise in what you are sharing and to whom so that the people in your audience feel like you are reading their minds when it comes to the messages they see from you. It's what allows someone to say, "This was meant for me."

Intimacy is the element of real, human connection in your marketing, and it's the piece that I feel entrepreneurs miss the boat on the most. Nothing makes business happen and money move faster than trust. And the fastest way to build trust is through inviting others to share greater Intimacy with you.

You do this when you show up consistently to share value with your audience, when you are transparent and authentic in the messages you share, and when time is spent to build actual relationships with the people in your audience. When you foster real connections with people (and even better when you facilitate an active community for them to engage in), you will be floored by how much easier sales are to make.

This is what allows someone to say, "This person is like me, I want to work with them." It's nothing new. People have always been more willing to say yes, say it faster, and be less price resistant when dealing with someone they already know, like, and trust.

When you combine all three of these key elements, something amazing happens. What that is will become clear in the coming pages, starting with a closer look at Relevance, where you'll learn how to make sure *every* message you send out speaks clearly and powerfully.

RELEVANCE AND ITS IMPORTANCE

While I officially launched and shared The Relevancy, Omnipresence and Intimacy Marketing & Sales Method publicly in April 2018, the seeds for it were being planted for *years* before it all came together. Before The Relevancy, Omnipresence and Intimacy Marketing & Sales Method, I had something called The SSF Method, a method for understanding the Mindset of those who want to buy your products and services. It stood for The Sidewalk, Slow Lane, Fast Lane Method and it came to me while reading M.J. DeMarco's book *The Millionaire Fastlane*. I took his concepts around generating wealth and applied them specifically to marketing.

The SSF Method is quite simple in that it states that *everyone* in your market falls into one of three buckets:

1. THE SIDEWALK

People on the Sidewalk are not ready to buy what you have to offer. So much so that any sort of message about your offer, product, or solution will be ignored. In fact, Side-walkers often are *not even aware* that they have the pain or problem that you help solve. While the symptoms of the problem are showing up in their business or their relationships or their health or in other areas of their life, they simply don't feel it, think about it, or perceive it to be *that bad*. Either that or they are currently resigned to the belief that it's the way it is and that there is nothing that could be done for it to change *for them*.

For someone on the Sidewalk to move to the Slow Lane, they need education, illumination, insight, or revelation. They need to clearly see that the problem exists and begin to understand how much it is costing them to allow the problem to persist. Once that happens, they are now problem-aware and become open to finding the right solution for them to take care of it.

2. THE SLOW LANE

Humans are hardwired to want to solve problems. Once a person becomes *truly* aware of a problem (and sees how it is creating unwanted outcomes in their life), they start looking for ways to resolve it, even if only on a subtle, subconscious level at the start.

While Slow Laners aren't yet actively hunting for and vetting potential solutions, they are now receptive to consuming messages about potential solutions. These messages are now Relevant to them. Even with this increased openness, it still isn't yet time to really start selling your offer. What needs to happen here for Slow Laners is they want to know there is some sort of proven method or process that has worked for other people with the same problem to solve it. They are looking for an authority they can trust to help them bridge the gap between where they are and where they want to be. This is a huge part of why your positioning is so important and is something we'll dive into later in this section.

As someone in the Slow Lane spends more time thinking about and feeling the problem and the more a viable potential solution presents itself, they then accelerate into the Fast Lane.

3. THE FAST LANE

Once someone can understand their problem and can see a potentially viable solution, they are firmly in the Fast Lane. But people don't stay in the Fast Lane for very long. It would be too painful and emotionally draining to stay in a spot of being highly ready to do something about a problem but not actually doing something about it.

One of two things will happen: they're going to research, vet, and ultimately choose a solution, or they're going to convince themselves that the problem isn't *that bad* right now, to the point where they decelerate back into the Slow Lane. This means that you have a limited window of opportunity to effectively present *your* solution that will satisfy them both logically *and* emotionally, and position you as *the* authority who has the method that is best suited to solve this problem for them.

A major mistake I see entrepreneurs make is that they market too heavily to the Fast Lane. At any given point, only about 3 percent of your market is actively in the Fast Lane, and sending too many Fast Lane messages to people who are in the Slow Lane or Sidewalk will make them tune *you* out and categorize you as irrelevant in their minds before they even arrive in the Fast Lane.

Here, you can see the full SSF Method Messaging Matrix. This will help you figure out exactly which kinds of messages to send, who to send them to, and when.

As my understanding and experience with The SSF Method grew, it started to become clear that the entire method fell under the umbrella of Relevance. It's about always sending out *Relevant* messages to the right people at the right time. It's about having the right message, the right positioning, and the right offer for your market.

While The SSF Method became a fairly famous method in the marketing community, through time, I realized it was a SMALL part of a very important framework.

Now that we have a strong framework for *what* Relevance is, let's dive into a bit of the *how*.

RELEVANCE = MESSAGING, POSITIONING, AND OFFER

The SSF Method helps give a framework for how to send the right message at the right time, but there's a lot more to being Relevant than just that.

I'm sure you've seen entrepreneurs who have large social media followings and tons of people who consume every message they send out, but despite that, they struggle when it comes time to convert the attention into sales and revenue. This happens a lot with influencers, all of the time. They've got the messaging down but there's a disconnect in either their positioning or in their offer (or in both). This disconnect usually happens when an entrepreneur hasn't thought enough about what they present to their market.

You *can't* be Relevant if you are unclear in communicating **who you are** and **what you have to offer**. If someone can't understand that what you're offering is *specifically for them*, there is no chance they're going to give it the time of day, *especially* when there is a near infinite number of other things competing for their attention. Even if what you *truly* do for people is intricate and complicated, you need to figure out a way to share a simple, clear value proposition with your market. Very few people are going to undertake the research necessary to get to the bottom of something intricate or complicated, and good luck selling something that people don't believe is for them or if they don't understand the core outcome(s) of what you're offering.

Many entrepreneurs say it feels painful and limiting to get down to such a level of precise clarity in exactly *what* they are offering and exactly to *whom* they are offering it, but those who brave facing that discomfort come to understand the value of the exercise soon after committing to it. And I totally get why so many entrepreneurs shy away from doing this exercise. When you're stuck on the hamster wheel, it is *much* harder to make long-term choices. Resolving to stick to an avatar can be a struggle when you have bills that *need* to get paid, so you end up settling for less than perfect clients (which end up costing you significantly in some way or another *eventually*).

There also are some potential scarcity issues here because if you *do* commit to an avatar, you'll start saying no to some clients that you previously would have said yes to, which means less money flowing into the business. And while that *is* true in the short term, you'll soon see that *only* working with *your* best type(s) of client brings a handful of valuable benefits:

- Your working relationships with clients are smoother,

easier, and ultimately more profitable, as they require less of your business's resources to serve them well.

- Because of this, your business can serve *more* perfect clients than it can imperfect clients (opening the door for overall higher revenue *and* profitability).
- Working with your clients is a source of energy, fulfillment, and growth for you.
- You will be able to build a better business with optimization for the exact customer you're serving.
- People will get to know you for helping that type of person, which will allow you to position yourself for more and more of those clients.
- If you want to become famous and a Top 100, or even 500 in your industry, this is a must.

Similarly, many entrepreneurs don't give enough conscious thought to how their messages are building or detracting from the power of their position in the minds of people in their market. This one is a lot harder to measure (especially because there is usually a lag time between making a positioning improvement and when you begin to reap the rewards from it).

POSITIONING

Positioning is sort of like sex when you're sixteen—you know you want it; however, you really don't have much ability to understand how to get it, or at least that's how I felt. Positioning, I've found, is determined by four separate things that take the ambiguity out of the equation and allow for a systematic way to actually be seen in the marketplace the way you wish.

1. Your Unfair Advantage

Back in 2013, at one of the businesses I started, our tagline was "We amplify your unfair advantage." Since then, the word has become far more popular (not by much of my own doing). However, in one of my most popular articles (and maybe someday a book), I talk about how to find your unfair advantage.

See, I believe that your unfair advantage is a massive part of your positioning, simply due to the fact that if you do not include it, you include the one piece that no one else can copy: your unique skill, talent, knowledge, expertise and process. Further, as you'll see later in this book, our customers are yearning for an intimate connection with you, and when we push this as part of our positioning, we're able to actively and accurately engage who we want to work with. Remember, Relevancy as a whole is about attracting the **Perfect Clients.**

Now, how do you extract your Unfair Advantage? Well, here's the six key areas and what I've found as the easiest way to extract this so you can use it inside of your marketing and ensure you become Relevant.

1. Experience

Everything that's happened to you in the past happened to you and only you—the good, the bad, the boring. It's led you to the person you are today, and it's unlike anyone else. Use these experiences to your advantage. Share the stories unique to you. Nobody else has them, and although there are many people who can do what you do, nobody can tell the same story.

So right now, write down three meaningful experiences that had a big impact on your life. Good or bad, it does not matter. These experiences open you up to the world and allow your unfair advantage to shine through.

Take me, for instance, and my story about slipping into a million dollars in debt or the story of me blowing up a successful business. This is a tough story to share, but it's also one of the most powerful. I've built immense trust by sharing this experience, and although other people can do what I can, nobody has this story. It's unique to me, and it's part of my unfair advantage.

2. Skills

You have skills that few other people don't. Many may have similar businesses as you, share the same space and provide a similar solution, but few possess the same skills you do.

One of my unique skills is my ability to show up and become omnipresent. There are other people who offer what I do, and many of them are better writers, better speakers, and better on video, but few are as good at being Relevant to the right people, at the right time. I've nurtured this skill over fifteen years, and today, it sets me apart from everyone else. It forms part of my unfair advantage, so the question now is: What are your unique skills?

Spend a few minutes thinking about this, and write down three skills you have that nobody else does. They don't have to be businesses related, because so long as they're unique to you, they'll help you amplify your unfair advantage.

3. Talent

Everyone is born with certain talents, and unlike skills (that you learn), most of your talents come somewhat naturally to you.

One of mine is my ability to connect the dots and come up with big ideas before anyone else. This allows me to jump on trends before they become trends and create solutions for complex problems. This comes naturally to me. I don't spend much time or energy doing it. I find it easy, whereas other people find it impossible.

Like me, you have certain talents that come easy to you. So

once again, write down three talents that come naturally to you, and that separates you from the rest. These form part of your unfair advantage that nobody else can touch.

4. Knowledge

Over the years, you have consumed a great deal of knowledge that other people haven't. Through books, mentors, courses, and everything else, you have created a body of knowledge that plays a role in your unfair advantage. Often, you don't even realize you know what you know. You take it for granted and assume other people know it too. For me, this largely focuses around online marketing and scaling businesses from six to seven figures.

I've done it for years and take the knowledge I've developed for granted. But this knowledge sets me apart from most other people and allows me to serve my audience in a big way.

You, too, have created a body of knowledge, so write down three things you know that most people don't. This allows you to take what you do to the next level and to unleash your unfair advantage on the world.

5. Character

Each day, you develop your character. Every good, bad, and

indifferent situation affects your character, and over the years, it's led you to the person you are today. Your character depends on who you surround yourself with and your environment (now and in the past), and the great thing about your character is that it attracts certain people and repels others.

Personally, I repel a lot of people. I have my haters, and although this is sometimes hard to accept, it's a good thing. Why? Because it allows me to further attract the right kind of person.

Your character does the same. It attracts some and repels others, and all this allows you to use your unfair advantage to become the go-to person for those you serve. So write down three character traits that are unique to you. Don't worry about pushing certain people away, as they weren't a good fit anyway.

6. Connections

The people you know play a fundamental role in your unfair advantage. Those you trust—and who trust you—open doors that will not open for other people. Your connections count. So write down three influential connections you have that will help you expand your unfair advantage.

Together, these six steps form the foundation of your unfair advantage. If you've gone through each step and made notes where I asked you to, you now have eighteen points to work with that not only help you discover your unfair advantage but that you can then unleash on the world.

Your unfair advantage forms the DNA of who you are as an entrepreneur and, as such, the DNA of your business. There's too much competition to try and be and look like everyone else. You need to be you, and you need to use your unfair advantage so nobody else can replicate it.

Once they've seen this on paper, most people I work with actually see themselves for the first time or, at the least, more clearly than before.

Your unfair advantage, in relation to your positioning, allows for your ideal client to also see this version of you, as I believe if **you can't see you, then it's difficult for others.** And in a sea of online advertising and muddy waters where everyone may look the same, this allows you to extract quickly why you're different and then integrate that into the business.

Whenever I dive into the DNA of Relevancy, it always comes down to this. I mean, why is it that you can take two completely different people who have the same type of product and one will outsell the other? Or create technology that is seamless? Or perhaps, you see two speakers on stage.

One really resonates and vibes with you well, and the other doesn't, yet the one that didn't got a standing ovation?

The unfair advantage is a lot less about what you can compare yourself to in the marketplace and a lot more about who you are going to naturally attract, because your DNA inside of Relevancy is based upon your unfair advantage. It's important to understand this.

When I presented this onstage back in 2014 at a conference, everyone loved it, and while I had no idea at the time I would use it in an ongoing basis, here's the simple way to understand your unfair advantage so that it empowers you to use it inside of everything you do—from marketing to sales to customer service and delivery. Once I realized that this is what our potential customers YEARN for, it made things MUCH easier.

About two years ago, I was developing a marketing campaign. At this point in the history of my business, I had far more resources then I was used to—writers, designers, a creative director, tech implementers. Far away from the days of me inside of a landing page editor and an email system. I had a great marketing campaign idea. I brought it to the team, and I let them go with it. What happened next blew my mind.

See, we tested this campaign beforehand with my copy, my

terrible graphics, everything from me. And it did extremely well. We pushed online the version that my team created, which probably cost us $30,000 to produce. The results were terrible. I mean, we didn't even break even. Why was that? In my reflection, I realized a key flaw that is important in ensuring that you're Relevant—even more as you're scaling your business to eight figures and beyond. Your Relevancy is **so** tied to your unfair advantage that if your team and you yourself don't understand it, then it can't be replicated.

Ever have a Facebook post that didn't get likes? An email blast that fell flat? A sales call that wasn't just you? A marketing campaign that just sucked? If you look at these occurrences, typically, it's because you haven't extracted and replicated your unfair advantage.

In this advertising campaign, we did professional with fancy graphics, amazing copy, all the things that should convert. Yet, when we went to use it, it didn't look like me. It amplified their PAIN, but didn't create a point of Relevancy with my personality. And considering that people buy from people they feel connected with, it failed. The lesson? Extract your unfair advantage and use it in everything you ever do.

2. Your Method/Unique Process

A friend of mine, Todd Herman from the *90 Day Year*, told

me this. I'm paraphrasing. *The difference between an expert and a thought leader, is the thought leader has developed a specific method so that people can understand the context, not just the information they share.* Of course, Todd also helped me secure the pieces required for The Relevancy, Omnipresence and Intimacy Marketing & Sales Method and The Nuclear Effect, and since using them as a methodology, my core business grew by 500 percent in less than six months.

Now, the beauty of a method is that it allows you recognition inside of your industry **that isn't tied directly to you as an individual.** Think about it this way: you have a personal brand, your business has a brand, and your method has a brand. This has led the way for me to create an eight-figure business on the back of The Relevancy, Omnipresence and Intimacy Marketing & Sales Method, which has also helped my own personal brand, investment opportunities, and everything under the sun.

Further, this gives you the ability to do three core really cool things:

First, it allows you to go to market and attract people by showing them the path of redemption without first having to have them buy into you or your brand. In my work, I've found that it's much easier to get someone to buy into The Relevancy, Omnipresence and Intimacy Marketing & Sales Method and my processes that have built million-dollar companies than it is to get them to buy into my bald mugshot.

Second, it allows you to start building a business that, at some point, can be sold or, at the least, has the ability for you to step away or not be the CEO.

And lastly, it allows you to effectively build a business that doesn't have to have you included in the delivery of what you sell.

In short, having a method allows you to build a sustainable business that can live without you, and in the marketplace, it allows you to attract your ideal, perfect customer by showing them the path going from pain to redemption, ensuring that they don't have to fall in love with you or your brand first.

The next question that I hear every single time that I bring this up: Scott, how the heck do I develop a method? Well, I've developed a super simple strategy that will allow you to extract your method and experiment with it in real time. Keep in mind, I'm not saying that it'll work perfectly. The Relevancy, Omnipresence and Intimacy Marketing & Sales Method took three years for it to be discovered, and in many ways, a method is a continual work in progress.

However, here's the best way I know how to develop a

method. First, you must realize that a methodology is what you have right now. Every single time that you work with anyone inside of your business, you have a specific method that you use in order to achieve an intended result. All we are doing is extracting this method, allowing for it to be contextualized, and then being named in an easy-to-use framework so that people don't throw their hands up.

At a one-day event I held once, Joel asked, "How do I find that process?"

I responded with, "Do you record your client calls when working with them?"

He said yes and then smiled.

See, our process and method is embedded inside of who we are because you're likely really good at what you do, and if you don't believe you have a method, consider this. If you don't have a method, it means you aren't good at what you do.

Second, once you've come to this realization, you need to write step by step exactly what you do and what makes up the unique process that you bring someone through. This may be long or short; however, once you do, you'll start seeing things that can be grouped.

For example, the R in R.O.I. came from the fact that the

SSF Method was no longer adequate based upon realizing that all three pieces are required. I realized that the SSF Method was in reality messaging, and that messaging without position ended up told to deaf ears, and further, even if you had those two, if you didn't have the right offer inside of alignment, no one would give you their money.

Now, I discovered this by looking at what I did when I privately mentored someone. Each and every time I would dive into their avatar, I would understand the position in the marketplace. Further, I would help them craft their DNA into a method and then help them typically clarify their offer. Of course, it was far more fragmented. In reality, I didn't realize I was helping them craft an offer. I just wanted to help them make more money. I didn't see it as helping them with their avatar. I simply wanted to ensure they could sell to the right people. I didn't see it as the fact I was helping them with messaging. I simply was helping them implement the three core marketing lanes inside of The SSF Method.

See, we've already developed the constructs of our method; it's simply the fact that we haven't extracted it. So now you see your process and you're starting to group pieces. The core thing that you must realize is that this is a work in progress. At the beginning, it may not be sexy (sort of like my first method, called The SSF Method); however, in time, it can become extremely sexy.

The next part is where the rubber hits the road. Without naming the method, you'll want to start testing it in conversation, first with your clients, then with potential clients and listening for real-time feedback. Instead of saying, "Hey, what do you think of this?" it's more of a conversation where you lead with confidence and are looking for body signals, tone, or confusion/clarity. You'll quickly hear these cues and will continue to refine the method.

Now the next part comes, which is either writing about it, having a presentation, such as a webinar, or selling with it. Again, the method doesn't need a name just yet (typically names aren't easy); rather, you're simply just applying your process and showing others how you do things. As you'll discover, this method is a core part and will become a core part of your strategy moving forward, yet it's an ever-morphing aspect of your business and intellectual property.

As time moves on, you'll see what works more and more, which is where the refining process is. For example, this book started as being just Relevancy, then Relevancy and Omnipresence, and then it turned into R.O.I., and then the resultant turned into The Nuclear Effect. This was a many-month process of various conversations, webinars, emails to tens of thousands of people and real-time feedback of what worked and what didn't.

Overall, if you even just start with your process, you'll find that, over time, it'll take on a life of its own, and you'll discover your own method, allowing you to use the power of what a method does for you inside of positioning. The graphics will come later. The sexy bits will come later. Just get it on paper and get it in front of people. It'll develop itself if you just have the confidence for the first version.

3. X Does Y. You Need to Know Him Because Z

People will only remember a small fraction of who you are and what you do until Omnipresence is implemented, which creates the ability for more information to be retained due to more impressions of who, where, what, how, and why that came from you or your brand.

As Maya Angelou said, "I've learned that people will forget what you said, people will forget what you did, but people will never forget how you made them feel."

This requires us to be extremely clear, which is why I love this framework. If someone was introducing you, what would they say? X does Y. You need to know him because Z.

For example: Scott helps entrepreneurs scale to seven figures and beyond. You need to know him because it sounds like you have an opportunity for sales and marketing growth.

How do you extract this? First, forget what you think you

do. What you're really attempting to formulate is what other people need to know that you do. In doing this for those I've served, I've typically looked at who they've served, the greatest pain they solve and can find the perfect intro as Clay Hebert talks about by using the gap that they solve between the pain and vision for their customers.

Take what you have, then write it out thirty times. Scrap what you've written and start again. This time, much simpler. I'm talking, QUICK. You have such a small attention span. Further, if there is jargon, it's useless. If an eight-year-old doesn't get it, someone on the internet scrolling for five seconds won't either.

At this point, someone understands your method, they understand your unfair advantage, and they understand specifically what you do. The next piece of positioning?

4. The Story

Craft a story that someone will care about. A brand story is extremely powerful. Human beings, since we've been human, have connected deeply based upon one person telling the other a story.

As humans, I believe we are natural seekers. It's what nearly everyone will do until someone gives up on seeking and because, unfortunately, a lot of the world has given up on the search. It allows us to capture attention by developing brand stories.

I don't consider myself an expert in crafting brand stories. If I'm honest, I've always discounted this part of the positioning strategy. For the longest time, while I would have my clients go through this process, I never would myself. I always thought, *If I'm good, people will follow me.* See, that doesn't work.

In our digital age, we will give Relevant attention to those in which we can connect to via their stories, which allows us to vicariously live through them. Think about it. All of social media consumption is people following others, allowing them to disconnect from their current reality and live in someone else's. With the rise of virtual reality in the next few years, you will see more and more of this.

Don't get me wrong, I'm not an advocate of this. I simply know that Relevancy's missing component is the ability for your potential customers to look at you and want to be you, or rather, want to be what your brand stands for.

Why is influencer marketing so big? Why did social media get so big? Why has all of this internet stuff created so much momentum? Deep down, I believe as a society, we are asleep. And we will give our attention to whoever resonates with us the most and who isn't asleep.

Your brand story is by far one of the most important parts, and while you and me both might get sick of telling the same stories over and over. Everyone, from political figures that seemingly had no chance of getting elected to the best gurus in the world have done an incredible job of creating Relevant stories, which draw in our desire to seek an adventure—even if we AREN'T the one's exploring, ourselves.

There's plenty of ways to develop your brand story. I've had the story-selling gurus give me plenty of exercises; however, I'll give you the simple way that has always worked for me. Write every single story dialogue you can think of that is important to you, or to your customer, that is based on your brand or your personal life.

For me, it's things like throwing a birthday party and no one showing up. It's about going into massive debt, while having successes in the past. It's about going nomadic to find myself, then finding my soulmate.

This is a document that may end up being ten pages long, or two. However, now that you have a variety of stories, you want to organize them from highs to lows. This will become your go-to for creating content (as we'll talk about in the Omnipresence section of this book). From here, you'll create an overall story.

Personally, I've found that doing a video, even a live stream on this, then converting this to text is the best. As a rule of thumb, if you truly want to nail personal story and Relevance, authenticity is your friend.

Our world thrives on transparency; as humans, we thrive on truth. As John Keats famously said, "Truth is Beauty and Beauty is Truth." And as I've found, the more truth that we bring, the more Relevant we can be to the people who need to know that we are here to help them, connect with them, and help them toward their vision.

This process doesn't need to be difficult or long. Rather, it's a set of stories that make up your brand story, with an overview of the core brand story. Now, if you've done this brand story process and it involved your unfair advantage, you were authentic in the way that you translated your stories. If you talk to others about your story, you should have the look of "whoa."

It **doesn't matter** if you are amazed by your brand story. All that matters is if your authentic tone is being understood, valued, and believed by your avatar and core audience that allows for driven action. If you aren't intentional with how you position yourself, then you leave it completely up to chance as to how others perceive you, your authority, your ability to get results, and how valuable your offers are.

As you can see, inside of marketing, there is a lot to unpack.

In essence, Relevancy is a combination of your positioning, avatar, messaging, and offer coming together. Think of it this way:

- If you speak to the right avatar, but have the wrong positioning, they won't trust you.
- If you have the wrong offer, they won't see it as valuable, for who they are.
- If you have the wrong messaging, they won't get it and you won't get their attention.

These create the perfect Relevancy, which is one of the most important pieces of marketing. Without Relevancy, being able to attract attention toward your signal is nearly impossible.

Speaking of, let's put a wrap on the Relevance section by covering how to create a powerful, compelling offer that speaks directly to those who you most want to work with. And when I say "offer," it doesn't have to be things that you're selling for money. It could also be things you're offering for free in exchange for their email address or what you're offering to share with them in exchange for an hour of their time by attending your webinar.

Regardless of whether the cost is their time or their money, people need to be thoroughly compelled by an offer in order to take action on it. As mentioned earlier, the first step is clarity. A mistake a lot of entrepreneurs make is falling prey to the curse of knowledge. Meaning that because *they* so deeply understand every piece of their offer, they actually forget what it is like to have absolutely no context on the offer. Because of that, the messages sent about the offer miss the mark just a little bit, and as a result, a lot of would-be buyers wind up passing on an opportunity that would have really helped them (had they been clear on how the offer was Relevant to them).

There are four questions you need to ask yourself when you are crafting messages about an offer to make it Relevant:

Question 1: Who is this offer being made to?

If you've already created your avatar (your audience), then you know this answer well. And if you aren't yet able to precisely define your main avatar(s), I recommend investing an hour or so into doing it. Having this will make creating Relevant messages and offers *much* easier. It will also help you understand how to best position yourself in the eyes of the people you most want to serve.

Question 2: What is the core problem this offer is solving?

Once you're clear on *who* you are making your offer to, it's time to dive into the core thing they are really looking to have solved or transformed or upgraded in their life. The more you understand the problem, the symptoms of it, and the way it makes them feel to have to continue living with it, the better you can articulate how what you're offering can get them from where they are *now* to where they truly want to go.

The best way to deeply understand these things? Go out and do some customer research and development. Ask some probing, open-ended questions to some people who are in your market. Let them paint the picture of their internal landscape of thoughts and feelings in regard to the problem.

When you are able to do a good job of expressing the problem, what it looks and feels like, how they got there, and show a path to a better reality, you become incredibly Relevant to the people currently experiencing that problem. And when you are able to express it better than they can themselves, thereby giving them new insight into this thing that's been plaguing them, people see you as *the* solution (and selling them into your offer becomes incredibly easier).

Question 3: How are you actually solving this core problem?

Essentially there are two ways to go about sharing with people *how* you are going to help solve their problem.

One way is to share a laundry list of exercises, modules, and components of an offer. If you've ever had someone explain an offer to you that took minutes of them diving into the extreme details (and where your eyes glazed over within the first twenty-five seconds), then you know what I'm talking about. This is what happens when entrepreneurs don't have a signature process or methodology for getting results. Or rather, this is what happens when entrepreneurs haven't *clearly defined* what their signature process is and how it works at a high level.

Before people buy, they are far more interested in the bottom-line outcome and results. Once they're sold and believe *you* are the one to help them create those results, *then* they will be more open to the specific details.

Beyond that, people want to know there is a clear and proven process that reliably delivers those results. Think about it. Who are you going to trust more? Someone who has gotten successful results for *so many people* that they've been able to develop a methodology around delivering that result and/or solve that problem or someone who throws a whole bunch of features at you to the point that it feels overwhelming as opposed to an intentionally orchestrated process engineered to bring you a defined outcome, result, or benefit?

While the answer to that is easy to see, there is a deeper

implication of this distinction that most entrepreneurs (even savvy ones) don't consider—*a lot* of your potential customers or clients will buy into *your method* before they will buy into you. Having a compelling framework shows them that there is a path to a better solution, and it paints the picture in their mind of the process they would go through if they invested in your offer.

If you're reading this book, there is a good chance that, on some level, you are in the business of transformation, even if you don't look at it that way. Whether you are transforming their business or their relationships or their Mindset or their health or...I could go on for a while. If you're not sure, most businesses that fall into the categories of coaching, consulting, training, events, speaker/influencer, or online courses are typically in the business of transformation.

When you show people that you have a precise, unique process for facilitating the transformation from where they are to where they want to go, and if the process makes sense to them (maybe even seeing it helps illuminate a new insight about their current circumstances), *that* will do far more to convert them into a believer in you than anything you could say about yourself (and when you pair that with an ever-growing amount of undeniable proof in your ability to deliver transformation in the form of other people's results and testimony, your momentum *really* starts to build).

And now that we're on the topic of transformation, let's look at the last question.

Question 4: What's the *most* transformation you *can* provide?

More and more businesses are finding themselves in the world of transformation. And when we are in the world of transformation, we have the opportunity to offer something powerful. So I want you to think about this question in two different ways:

A. Think about the *absolute most* transformation you could deliver to someone you worked with if you were compensated commensurately with the value you delivered them. I want you to think about something you believe you could charge six figures for, and if you already offer things at (or even beyond) six figures, then the challenge is to think about what *more* you could deliver (and what you'd charge for it).

Even if it feels completely unrealistic, this is an extremely valuable thought exercise. You're giving yourself a new context to explore, even if only for a few minutes. You're trying on a different pair of lenses through which you look at your business.

In the Product Pillar, one of the things we'll go over is how

to create one (or several) of these powerful, deeply transformative, and *very* high-ticket offers. For now, I just want
your mind to start opening to the idea. Then the other way
to think about this question is to:

B. Think about the most transformation you are able to
    deliver based on the price point of that particular offer.
    Business works best when everyone feels they were hon-
    ored and compensated fairly for what they contributed
    to the deal, which means that you feel that you were
    compensated well for the transformation you provided.

Let's say it costs your business $5,000 in time, energy,
expenses, and labor to deliver someone $100,000 of
value. Would you feel good if you were only paid $7,000
in exchange for the efforts (not to mention in exchange
for the results those efforts brought to the other person)?
I know I wouldn't! The key is to ask yourself what number
(or what range of numbers) *would* feel good for the different
levels of transformation you can help create or facilitate
for someone. Look to find that sweet spot where you are
delivering a powerful transformation with a high lifetime
ROI that *also* allows you to profit well from your efforts.

Once you feel solid about your Product offering(s), these
four questions above are the things that you need to answer
to send highly Relevant messages about those offers. Relevance strikes most powerfully when your audience can

see you positioned as an authority, sharing compelling messages *and* making compelling offers that feel like they were made for them.

Run a test in which you try being more direct about who you serve and how you serve them. Don't be surprised when you become strikingly Relevant to the *right* people. It's the difference between being a generalist and being a specialist. It's the difference between being an option versus being the option in your market.

If you don't know **who** you are serving, it is nearly impossible to craft a message that is Relevant enough for it to break through all the noise. Think about how clear and Relevant your message needs to be in order to command the attention of the people you want to reach among *every other competing priority, message, and stimuli* people have in their lives these days. Even if you only capture their attention for a few moments at first, it can be enough to get your foot in the door. That's enough. The O in The Relevancy, Omnipresence and Intimacy Marketing & Sales Method will take care of the rest.

As you can see, Relevancy isn't an easy process; however, once you nail it, you will have more customers who want to pay you what you're worth than you know what to do with. Heck, it's the reason I wrote this book. Most of the people who use The Relevancy, Omnipresence and Intimacy Marketing & Sales Method grew their business so quickly that they BROKE their entire business and had to transfer to the other pillars so they could keep growing.

OMNIPRESENCE

While Relevance was something that came through a lot of intentional thought and evolved over a couple years after starting as The SSF Method, Omnipresence was something I stumbled into by complete mistake.

Back in 2016 when I was really developing The SSF Method, I was shooting video and writing posts nearly every day. Unfortunately, this was right around the time Facebook really started to limit the organic reach of business pages. Back then, my ego was addicted to vanity metrics like views and likes and comments for my content. And it hurt my pride that I was pouring my creative energy into producing and sharing content, but only a fraction of people who I wanted to consume my content were even getting my stuff shown to them. It sucked.

After a week when I was *really* in the zone with the content I had created, I made the decision that it was going to be seen by my audience, no matter what. Even if it meant giving Facebook money in exchange for showing my content, I wasn't going to let my impact and my business results be dictated by the whims of their algorithm. And that's exactly what I did. My marketing budget shifted to include a significant portion of dollars going toward showing my (completely free) content to the people in my audience. It also made sense to me that there was *always* some marketing budget spent showing my stuff to completely new audiences (aka people who have never heard of me and are completely cold).

I did my best to target people I thought would find my stuff to be Relevant and spent ad dollars to show some content to them. The goal is to have an ongoing system for consistently generating new leads for your business and adding more people to *your* audience. Like I said, at first, I was just addicted to the view count, likes, and comments. However, what happened next blew my mind.

I started to become famous inside of this audience, this little bubble that I had built. My popularity was starting to rise. People were starting to see me in the position of a celebrity in the marketing and business arena. And people started offering me all sorts of interesting (and sometimes weird) opportunities. And all of a sudden it was much easier to be able to charge more money than I ever had before. I'm not talking a 15 percent increase in my rates. I'm talking about a 1,500 percent increase (in less than six months).

My one-on-one consulting fee quickly jumped from 5,000 percent with people saying yes faster and more enthusiastically at the higher rate than they ever did at the lower rate. With each sales call, I kept increasing the number to see how elastic the price actually was. Within a year, I had confidently stated $25,000/month as my fee on multiple sales calls with success. I had speaking engagements all over the world. Publishers wanted to create a book with me. Business deals came out of nowhere. People started to see my Relevant brilliance.

All of this was the unintentional result of really just wanting my content to be seen (so don't listen when people say that nothing good comes from just trying to gratify your ego!). I mistakenly fell into utilizing one of the most powerful marketing techniques that has been used by some of the most successful companies for the past couple centuries. I remember walking into a room of very high-end entrepreneurs—all multi-seven- and eight-figure entrepreneurs, and being a celebrity, talking about how they wanted to work with me.

From inside of this small bubble, people kept talking about me and the content I was producing, my methods, and the stories I would share. It blew me away. I hacked my way to the top of an industry in one-tenth the time it takes for most people, while not even spending that much money on marketing.

Omnipresence is EXTREMELY affordable and still is.

When I was introducing The Relevancy, Omnipresence and Intimacy Marketing & Sales Method to you, I mentioned that Intimacy is nothing new. Well, the same is true for Omnipresence. If you look at the most successful businesses in history as well as today, you'll realize they are *almost always* Omnipresent (at least to the people in their market). You can barely watch a TV, listen to a radio, or drive on a highway without being presented with an ad from the small handful of companies that dominate the auto insurance market (GEICO, State Farm, Progressive, and Allstate). In fact, while researching this book I discovered that this was written in the September 16, 1861 edition of *The New York Times*:

> Prominent among them was the *omnipresent* showman, PT Barnum, who had planned to make the occasion known far and wide, and their efforts were crowned with success.
>
> The city was fairly overrun with the almost numberless vehicles, while the railway station was crowded from morning far into the night.

Whether your business is as boring as car insurance or as exciting as the production put on by one of history's greatest showmen, effective Omnipresence will add to your bottom line and amplify the impact your business creates for others. GEICO operates in a very boring and very saturated market. There isn't much exciting or interesting about their product, and yet just about everyone (in the USA at least) can tell you what GEICO's value proposition is. In case you aren't familiar, their promise is that you can save 15 percent or more on your car insurance within fifteen minutes by calling GEICO. GEICO has found a way to share the same core message over and over and over (*for years*) in a way that remains fresh through innovative and entertaining messages that surround that consistent positioning, promise, offer, and value proposition.

Imagine if *everyone* in your market, niche, or field knew about your business and knew precisely what your business has to offer. What if they knew a lot about the kinds of results and case studies you've created? What if they knew a lot about you and your story? Imagine the greater depth of connection and Intimacy that would create between you and your potential clients. When this starts happening, don't be surprised when people start reaching out to you and deals start happening much faster because people already feel that they know, like, and trust you. They are *coming* to the conversation knowing who you are, knowing your value, your solution, your process, your method, and your historical track record of success. And you have a bit of a leg up because it is a near guarantee that your business is more interesting than GEICO's. *And*, unlike GEICO, you don't need a billion-dollar yearly advertising budget. You just need to be Omnipresent to your own small pond of people who you are *most* Relevant to.

Let's get back to the story of discovering this. My unintentional Omnipresence campaign was running for months and months before I realized what this strategy was *actually* doing and realizing that I had created a small pond of people who found my content to be Relevant, and then I became Omnipresent (but *only* inside of that specific pond of people). Essentially, I created a bubble where these people not only knew, liked, and trusted me, but I changed their belief systems, activated the Baader-Meinhof phenomenon (the effect where you feel as if you keep seeing something over and over again) along with a dozen other cognitive biases, including the confirmation bias, anchoring, framing effect, Barnum effect, the halo effect, optimism bias, group-think effect, spotlight effect, and the number of them go on.

See, I've always studied humans. The reason I'm a master at marketing is because I understand humans. Yet, what I didn't realize was, when you run an Omnipresence strategy long enough, the people in your pond will eventually have to make a binary decision. Because you keep showing up, they *have* to take a position.

They either end up REALLY liking you and become a true fan (which means not only will they likely buy what you offer, but they will recommend you, talk about you, and offer connections or opportunities to you). Or they will end up REALLY disliking you (which really means the worst they will do is ignore all your content or block your ads or leave a nasty comment).

When they see you so often, you have the opportunity to share more messages, strengthen your positioning, and fully articulate the value of your offer(s). When they see you so often, they start feeling kind of like they know you, and a strong connection starts to build. The value of your messages and the fact that you show up consistently speaks volumes with people and quickly builds trust.

Oftentimes, the people who like you end up *loving* you, while the people who don't like you usually will concede that they do *respect* you. Or as Grant Cardone simply stated, "Love me or hate me, you still know me." That sentiment is the crux of Omnipresence.

I've come across so many entrepreneurs who looked at advertising *only* as a way to drive sales. Or were gun-shy about spending money on advertising out of fear of not being able to earn an immediate return on the investment. Or thought that advertising in general is a bit gross or manipulative, so they stay away from it. And I wanted to address both of those here.

The first is if you have some negative associations with advertising as a whole, an effective Omnipresence strategy positions you to do *the exact opposite* of what most people judge and don't like about ads. Instead of hammering people with ads that are all trying to get people to buy something, a lot of Omnipresence ads aim to educate or illuminate or transform or evolve the people who are reached by the advertised message.

You've probably heard terminology around ads being served to people. Well, with an effective Omnipresence strategy, you truly are *serving* people through the ads and messages you are sending out. You are quite literally serving people through advertising and that, to me at least, is beautiful.

The second is around scarcity-based concerns of not earning an immediate return on the investment. One of the biggest Mindset shifts that needs to happen for someone to have consistent success with Omnipresence advertising is to understand the long term, invisible ROI that accrues as you continue to consistently serve people with ads.

As mentioned in the section on Relevance, only 3 percent of people are ready to buy *now* at any one given time. Omnipresence builds some invisible equity among the other 97 percent of your market. As those people accelerate from the Sidewalk or the Slow Lane into the Fast Lane, either you've laid a ton of groundwork with them *before* they were ready to position you to be the clear top option for them to choose, or you haven't.

Omnipresence creates a ton of value for your business that

simply is going to take several months (and in some cases a couple years) before it materializes into visible, tangible cash revenue. But make no mistake about it, that value was created *well* before the money arrived. It simply existed as invisible ROI that your Omnipresence efforts sowed for you that was waiting to be manifested as income.

If you truly understand the power of being able to serve people at scale through your ads combined with the incredible long-term ROI that comes with being Omnipresent (even if you can't *see* all of it just yet), you gain a massive advantage over the competition in your marketplace.

When you're implementing an Omnipresence strategy at the absolute *highest level*, the people in your audience simultaneously feel that you are reading their minds as well as feel that it was *completely their* own brilliant idea to pay you money to be able to work with you. But beware. Realize that when you're implementing an Omnipresence strategy at the absolute *lowest level*, you are simply turning people off at scale—spamming them with messages they don't care about—possibly burning your reputation (and *definitely* throwing your money down the drain) along the way.

However, when your Omnipresence strategy is filled with Relevant messages, you create a systematic way to show up at the right time in the right place to the right people. When you continue to do that for your audience, you become a celebrity and an authority to the people within your pond. When you have that kind of positioning, *everything* becomes easier. People will pay premium rates to work with you. Quality talent will want to join your team. People will want to do favors for you.

Trust me when I say that my life is *much* better post-Omnipresence than it was pre-Omnipresence. Now that we can clearly understand the theory behind Omnipresence and the incredible value it can create (both for your business and for the people you are being Omnipresent to).

The next step here is to go a bit into the *how* of Omnipresence. But unlike the *how* section of Relevance, it is nearly impossible to get into the nitty-gritty specifics of how to run an Omnipresence strategy in a book. It is technical, it's based on platforms, and it's ever-changing. Meaning, by the time you read this, it's likely that the technology that allows this to work won't work anymore.

What I can tell you in this book is this: Omnipresence comes down to being able to deliver your Relevant messages on the right platforms with the right frequency at the right time based upon the life cycle of your potential customer, along with their interest in what you've shown them beforehand, with combined intelligent segmenting.

In short, Omnipresence comes down to three core elements in your marketing:

1. TIMING

I talk about the right message at the right time, and it is the complete truth here. If you show the wrong messages at the wrong time, you are going to be annoying and not Relevant to someone. It's the core reason that I believe people MUST be Relevant before they are omnipresent, unless they want to burn every dollar they have.

For example, if you view a sales page and then you get an ad or message a day later with a "Did you mean to purchase this?" it might be Relevant. If you got the same message sixty days from now, would it be? Likely not.

The same SSF Methodology must be applied to Omnipresence. What messages must be delivered to someone at what time? If they are in the Slow Lane, it's different than the Fast Lane. If someone is on the sales page, it's different then if they just follow you on Instagram.

In life, timing is everything. The same goes for Omnipresence.

2. FREQUENCY

Too little, is too much. Too much, isn't enough. Frequency of someone seeing you is a second must inside of Omnipresence.

If someone stumbles across you and then you are everywhere, but that stumbling wasn't in-depth (for example: if they just visited your Instagram page). Then showing up in their life four times a day is probably a little much and will actually hurt your reputation and potential to turn that person into a customer.

Instead, frequency must be aligned to where someone is inside of your marketing, what they are viewing and how they are engaging with you.

Now, there's a fine line here. Many marketing gurus talk about behavioral marketing. This is based on if the person watched 25 percent of the video, show them another view. If they saw 50 percent of that one, show them a sales video.

I don't believe this is how humans work. Humans consume content in a less structured way, and we look for context. We don't watch full videos, and we skim words, we triple our audio speed. We are obsessed with speed and headlines.

So, when it comes to frequency, it's more about allowing for certain actions in your marketing to trigger different levels of frequency so that you become increasingly top of mind and in someone's orbit as they respond.

3. PLATFORMS

The final core element is platforms, which ones you'll use and at what times. From paid to organic and partnerships, there's a lot of different ways to be Omnipresent to someone. The more niche, the easier. The more Relevant, the easier. The smaller the audience, even easier.

At the beginning of your Omnipresence strategy, it might just be email or even text messaging. Soon, it might be Facebook, Instagram, YouTube, Google Display ads. The entire internet is accessible. And don't forget snail mail.

Omnipresence is the art of being everywhere while being Relevant. Now, trust me. This is ACTUALLY far easier than it sounds. And it mostly comes down to nuance and Relevancy.

However, beware. Those who are omnipresent without Relevancy have a BIG problem. They will spend MORE money, become a mosquito everywhere and annoying and have a NEGATIVE return on their investment.

Teaching this is *far* more effective when we can share some videos and some tools for managing the whole process. And you can find it here: www.thenucleareffect.com.

After stumbling upon the power of Omnipresence, I had the first two pieces of The Relevancy, Omnipresence and

Intimacy Marketing & Sales Method. And it would take several more months for the last piece of the puzzle to come into place.

INTIMACY

I want to talk about three very critical words that all start with C. More on that in a minute.

On a crisp California winter day, I was driving around the mountains of Malibu trying to clear my head a bit. I knew there was a missing piece to what I had been developing about how to effectively market in an online world that's become filled with a bunch of cold automation software, scarcity-driven messaging, and overall deception in order to try and boost sales.

Earlier that day, I was on a call with an incredibly successful entrepreneur who was a one-on-one client of mine, and he said, "Scott, I'm sick of all the automation in the marketing process and so are all of my customers. I just want intimacy back in the equation."

This conversation happened shortly after selling a company called Bots for Business to my friend Andrew Warner (best known as the founder of Mixergy). And I had learned *a lot* about Intimacy from creating, running, and ultimately selling that business. It showed me a little microcosm of the way so many businesses have been going over the past handful of years.

When you call a business these days, you often get an automated robot that answers (and often makes it quite difficult to get ahold of an actual human). When you give a business your email address, you get put into an automated sequence, and now we are seeing more and more chat bots, messenger bots, and AI-based marketing tools. And while it's all done in the name of efficiency and productivity, there is nothing Intimate about a robot. And that's fine for lower ticket products, but if you're selling a higher ticket, higher touch, transformational offer, then it is a complete mismatch to try to invite someone into working Intimately with your business by selling them through automations and robots.

From the very start, treat people in the way you want them to relate to your business, meaning that if you want them to really trust and connect with you, robots and automation aren't going to cut it. If you want people to trust you to help solve significant pains in their business or their relationships or their health or in another major area of their life, if you want people to vulnerably share the ugly truths of their current situation, courageously let you see into their dreams and aspirations, and pay you a significant amount of money to help them shift from the former to the latter, *you* need to lead with Intimacy.

As people try to scale their businesses, they think they need to reduce Intimacy in order to grow their business. And this is one of the main reasons why entrepreneurs struggle when trying to scale, they end up losing a bit of the magic that really drew people to them in the first place.

When it comes down to it, human beings *crave* connection, conversation, and community (those being the three C's of Intimacy). When you're selling transformation, people need to trust you before they're going to entrust you with helping them with something important, valuable, and potentially vulnerable to them.

If you can't connect with them at all *before* they pay you money, they're not going to pay you any money. If you don't make time to have a conversation with someone where they feel seen and met where they are now (while also feeling your confidence that you can help deliver them to where they want to go), it's going to be much harder to get people to pay you any money.

And while community isn't quite the necessity that connection and conversation are, having a community of people built around your business will inspire a lot of trust among your potential clients (while also serving as a breeding ground for some great connections and conversations).

We are more connected than ever and yet people are more

starved for true connection than ever before. It's a huge part of why depression is on the rise (especially younger people who don't know anything other than our hyperconnected world—a world devoid of the bonds that actually create Intimacy).

Not only is Intimacy the thing that actually makes money move, you have an opportunity to really touch people through your business. I've had conversations both online and in person where people have shared with me how meaningful the things I've shared have been to them. Even beyond business and marketing advice that helped them succeed on a higher level, people have told me they've changed the way they relate to their spouse, that they've forgiven themselves for things they've held shame around for years, or even overcame their addiction to pornography based on things I've shared.

That, to me, is priceless. I am actively grateful every day that I have an audience of people that I can share with, grow with, and make a meaningful impact on their lives.

CREATING CONNECTIONS, CONVERSATIONS, AND COMMUNITY

The first thing to know is that the overwhelming majority of businesses don't do *anything* to consciously build Intimacy or these three Cs into their business. Entrepreneurs avoid it partly because they don't always see the tie between action and result, and partly because it can feel a bit vulnerable, clunky, or awkward to build this kind of Intimacy with others as a business. I mean, it can be hard enough to be graceful in building and maintaining personal relationships before you throw in potential mental hang-ups around business, money, selling, etc.

So i want to start by saying that if you decide you're going to wait until you're *sure* that you're going to do this whole Intimacy thing perfectly, you're never going to start (thereby leaving a ton of potential revenue, connection, and impact on the table). Know that the only way to really nail this is through practice, implementation, and getting feedback to iterate off of.

If you see anyone who you think is great at these Intimacy pieces, it is because they are *well-practiced*. It isn't some natural gift that you either have or you don't. Even writing this gives me a little bit of imposter syndrome because of how many mistakes I've made along the way in trying to build Intimacy into my businesses. But the real truth is I am proud of myself for all the times I stepped up and gave it my best attempt even if the result wasn't what I wanted.

The book *Connections That Count: The Straight Talk Guide* shared how to host group lunch and dinner experiences for small- to medium-sized groups of people to connect with each other. And of course, you earn a ton of social capital when you play the role of host and connector.

BUILDING A COMMUNITY (AKA ETHICAL CULTURE BUILDING)

It doesn't matter how big your business is, being able to build a culture around it is critically important. It doesn't matter if this group is in person, on LinkedIn, Facebook, or even the comments section of your blog, every business has a brand, and every brand has a culture—most entrepreneurs allow the culture to just come instead of designing the culture.

Through Facebook groups, I've generated millions of dollars. No, I'm not talking about charging to be part of it, and I'm not talking about memberships either. I'm talking about free groups.

Back in 2013, I discovered Never Eat Alone by Keith Ferrizzia from Dan Martel (a brilliant entrepreneur friend of mine). In the next eighteen months, I hosted about 200 group lunches and dinners—in that time, I started to build a culture—through a free Facebook group. A year later, I had almost 1,000 people in that group, and it was POWERFUL. I hacked intimacy and authority by meeting over 1,000 (mostly new) people that were all entrepreneurs.

Fast-forward, and I've had many online groups that have

had tens of thousands of entrepreneurs inside of them, and they've been at the center point of many of my online businesses.

Why is it so important to have a community in your business? It's because your most captivated audience and human beings want to be part of a tribe, part of a group of people that have the same values, beliefs, and mission. People—your potential customers—will resonate with a group of people before they will resonate with you, your vision, your mission, your solution, or your product. And the interesting part? Them resonating with the community that you build—your cause or flagpole in the ground—allows for them to more easily become a customer later down the road and value your service or product even more.

Whenever I help create a community, I follow these ten rules for building a culture. While, I'm sure I could write a book just about communities after helping run so many, here's what I've found works as a framework:

TEN STEPS TO BUILDING A COMMUNITY

1. Define the difference you bring. What difference will you bring to the group that will entice people to join? What do you have to offer that is found nowhere else?
2. Who are the influencers and connectors you need? The first 100 people in your group should be influencers and

connectors who will advocate for you and bring others into the group. These should not be strangers.

3. Determine the exclusivity. You want to determine who gets access to your value. Yes, this will bother people, and you'll lose out on some business, but you want people who are going to value your exclusivity.

4. Determine your ideology. For your group to matter, you need to determine what you think is right and wrong. You need a clear perspective on what your ideas are and why you believe in them. People need to take a side on what you believe, or you're going to be around a lot of passive people.

5. Make members feel constantly appreciated. Whether through the content you produce or by reaching out to people, let people know that you truly appreciate them as members.

6. Make people feel like a better version of themselves. You want people to feel like a new, better version of themselves inside your group. You want them to feel like they are an improved version of themselves.

7. Create a common pain point. You need to determine what pain you and your group are solving. By giving people a common pain point, you can then present your solution.

8. Talk about your solution constantly. By constantly talking about and sharing ideas and resources related to the problem, you create high value in your group. You constantly help people solve the big pain point they're

stuck on. Create a methodology to overlay your ideology.

9. Let the advocates lead. There are going to be about seventy-five core people in your group who are in on everything. Let them lead the way in comments and threads. Let them speak up.

10. Show the big idea and vision constantly. People need to believe they are part of something bigger and better. They need to feel like they're empowered. By constantly giving them the big idea and vision, they will be on board with whatever you do.

Community (and creating Culture) does take a long time, and it does take work. However, if you want to build a business that can sustain the future, this will allow for better marketing, better Intimacy, and far more revenue per lead. It's what most don't do; thus, most fail.

As I mentioned earlier in this section, *you* need to lead with Intimacy and authenticity and vulnerability if you expect to really attract your people to you (whether that is getting someone to do something lower commitment, like joining your group, or something higher commitment, like buying your most exclusive product offering).

You see, there is *so much* content available out there on *every* possible topic that *you* are the main differentiator and unique value that you have to offer. By that I mean the sum total of your unique experience, talents, perspectives, character, and relationships. It honestly doesn't matter how good your content is at this point if people can't feel a Connection to *you*. Sure maybe the content is good and the people who consume it get value from it, but without that Connection, your content is simply a commodity. It is something that gets consumed and provides no further benefit (to them or to you) beyond the act of consumption.

When your messages are infused with some of *you* in it, when there are pieces about your story, your beliefs, your values, your experiences, your vision, or your heart that people can relate with, *that* is when your messages serve as true *assets* that provide a real, tangible Connection that will bring them back to you again and draw them into closer Intimacy with you.

In today's world, it is so easy for anyone to put out any message they want, regardless of whether it is true or not. It is so easy for anyone to present whatever image of themselves or their business or their results they want, regardless of whether it represents reality or not. And we've been trained to be distrustful of the things we see online.

Fortunately, there is something undeniable about consistent authenticity, transparency, and depth that *cannot* be faked. People often ask how they can be more authentic, more transparent, and share more of their depth in the messages they send out, and while it's kind of like the cliché dating advice of "Just be yourself," it's true. Of course, you have to know yourself a bit before you can really be yourself with some power and consistency.

So here is the main exercise that I recommend to you for getting clear on the things that will be meaningful for you to share about yourself and that will create a stronger sense of Connection for the people who see what you share. Sharing some of this can be *incredibly* difficult, and that is what makes it courageous and powerful. It is going where most people don't dare to go.

I remember when I first published my story of how I ended up being almost $1,000,000 in debt. It was one of the most difficult things I've ever done. I remember logging into my email system to take my mom off the email list before sending it out and then going straight to the shower to cry for the next two hours. In my mind, sending that email meant I admitted to everybody who knew me that I had failed, and I had to *really* look in the mirror to admit to myself that I had failed. It was a clear message that I don't have it all together and that I had made some serious missteps in business that led me to a difficult position.

Intimacy requires courage. It is difficult to allow yourself to really be seen (and potentially judged) by others. Yet what I have found is that the more honest and vulnerable I am, the more of me that I allow to be shared with others, the more I attract *precisely* the kinds of people I want to have around me.

This is true both personally and professionally. It was a handful of shares I made that inspired the woman who would become my wife to feel connected to me enough to reach out and start a conversation.

All kinds of new and wonderful things begin opening up for you and your business once you've got your Connection game on point and you're building your Community. From there, you're going to want to master the art of having effective Conversations with people that help convert them into customers and clients. And there is a way to do this mostly through social platforms that have a messaging feature like Facebook or Instagram before it is time to escalate to a phone call or video call. Because this truly is closer to the Sales Pillar of your business than the Marketing Pillar, we're going to save this for a section in the next chapter, which is all about Social Selling.

Regardless of whether someone has just recently Connected with you or whether they are an active member of your Community or whether they've reached out to have a Conversation with you, one of the biggest lessons I've ever learned about human behavior is that it is driven *way* more by feelings than it is by thoughts; it is driven by emotions over intellect.

The world is *full* of options for people to choose from when they want to invest in the kind(s) of things you offer. There are plenty of directly competing options as well as tons of indirect competing options. What I mean is that by choosing *you*, they are choosing you over *every* other possible option available to them (including doing *nothing* about their current situation). Instead of hiring a coach or consultant, someone can buy a book or an online course or go to a workshop or hire an employee to try to solve the problem(s) they're looking to solve.

It's almost impossible to get someone to take action toward something they are indifferent toward. That means that your potential client needs to *feel* how much their problem is costing them (covered in Relevancy), and they need to *feel* Connection to you in trusting that you are *the* option for them among a sea of potential choices.

The more Intimacy that is built between you and your audience, prospects, and clients, the easier and faster everything will be for your business. Business happens at the speed of trust. And I mean more than just the direct action of someone paying you money.

You'll be able to get more (and more honest) feedback from people, you'll be able to validate new ideas faster, you'll have more true fans who will consume (and share) your messages, and a steady flow of people looking to give you value (because you've given so much to them). On top of all that, your life will be richer on all levels when you have more genuine Connection and impact. We live in a world that is being increasingly run by automations and robots, but this technological evolution has *far* outpaced human evolution.

Tap into the deepest things that we *all* crave as human beings. Create Intimacy through more Connection, Conversation, and Community, and watch how it *completely* changes your business.

WHEN YOU CREATE MARKETING ABUNDANCE

While The Relevancy, Omnipresence and Intimacy Marketing & Sales Method is not the *only* way to create marketing abundance, I've found it can get your business there with greater speed, efficiency, and effectiveness than anything else. (It's why this Pillar in itself was over 10,000 words. There is a lot of power *and* a lot of nuance in the method.)

Once you start putting each of the pieces of The Relevancy, Omnipresence and Intimacy Marketing & Sales Method to work in your business, you'll begin to see more leads and better opportunities being attracted to you. When you *know* you will *always* have good options available to you in business, you can start doing more strategic long-term thinking. You can invest with more confidence into the other areas of your business and have a defined plan for *sustainable* growth.

Having this is the first step toward really being able to unleash The Nuclear Effect in your business. And the *second step* is to be able to consistently enroll this abundance of leads into deals through your sales efforts, which brings us to our second Pillar: Sales.

To access the resources for this chapter, visit: www.thenucleareffect.com/resources/.

CHAPTER 5

PILLAR #2: SALES

Sales is the ultimate moment of impact in business.

Even if your marketing is great, your product delivers the promised result like clockwork, and you have a world-class team ready to serve clients, people still need to be sold and enrolled into making a clear decision to say yes to what you are offering. Regardless of what you may think, people need the sales process, and it's a time of radical transformation in someone's Mindset and momentum. Without it your potential customers will stay in the Slow Lane or Fast Lane forever, simply not solving the problems in their life that you solve.

This section is going to show you a bit of how you can set yourself up for sales success (all the way from the first time someone hears about you to all the way through reenrolling past clients into new offers). It starts with understanding the impression your business makes on people and how they view your business in comparison to the other options they have in your marketplace.

THE POWER OF POSITIONING

Most entrepreneurs think of sales as contained in the actual sales conversation(s) had with a potential client, but the truth is that the sale starts *way* before a sales call is ever even scheduled. In fact, your Sales Pillar is ***intimately*** tied to your Marketing Pillar (as well as to your Product Pillar). The quality of your marketing determines both the number of sales opportunities you have flowing to you as well as the quality of those leads.

If we were to compare business to the game of golf, marketing is the long game (i.e., your driver and your irons) and sales is the short game (chipping and putting). The better your marketing is, the shorter and easier your putts become in order to make sales. Those who understand this, also understand that the better your marketing, the easier it is for your sale tools—such as webinars, sale letters, or you selling your service, to do your job.

Think: if marketing does its job, your close rate will be MUCH higher, and the process won't feel salesy because you won't have to convince that there is a pain, problem, method, or your authority.

See: **It's really *all* about positioning.** If you're getting questions like this: So exactly what do you do? What results do people get from working with you? How does this program work? Do you have any past clients I can talk to about their experience working with you before I make a decision? These kinds of questions mean that your marketing can be improved to better inform people about you, your program, your results, etc. *before* they get on the phone with you.

Your marketing can help you further improve the *positioning* you have in the mind of your prospect when they get on the call with you.

Think about how much time is wasted on sales calls answering questions like the ones above, having to explain who you are, and having to defend your value to people. Infusing your marketing with Relevance, Omnipresence, and Intimacy will make all of your sales *much* easier to close. Relevance captures peoples' attention. Omnipresence keeps their attention and informs them about who you are, your results, your value, etc. (so these parts never have to be addressed on sales calls ever again). Intimacy draws people closer to you and opens them up to having a sales conversation with you. And positioning can help set you up for success *before* the sales process begins.

This coming section is about how to successfully close the deal on a higher percentage of your sales opportunities.

THE FOUR-STEP CLOSE FOR EFFORTLESS, ETHICAL ENROLLMENT FOR YOUR PROGRAMS AND SERVICES

Once you have your positioning down, closing sales becomes much easier because you aren't selling yourself—you're selling the future version of your potential customer back to them. You aren't important; they are. And while you can't change the power and impact of your positioning overnight, you can change your sales call and closing strategy in an instant.

I want to share with you the most effective sales process I've discovered so far. It's helped me generate millions of dollars in revenue, approaching over $20 million in sales in a very short period of time. This Four-Step Close was taught to me by my friend Jesse Elder, and since then, it's completely transformed how my sales team and I run our sales calls.

In reality, it's not a script; it's a flow of being able to become curious. I believe that effective selling is the intersection of curiosity, vibration, empathy, and coaching. See, most people think of selling as pitching. Yet, if your marketing has worked, it's actually the ability to see the world from the lens of the person on your phone.

This creates a really interesting effect inside of your sales—regardless if they purchase or not, the sales process is creating a transformative state from where someone wants to be to where they are. Simply put, regardless if they invest or not, you've helped them. I believe that's important in business and life. Plus, they'll buy in the future: #playthe-longgame. Here's how it works.

STEP ONE: ILLUMINATE YOUR POTENTIAL CLIENT'S PAIN

Your first step is to help your prospect more clearly understand their current pain so they can really see and feel how much these problems are costing them, holding them back, and preventing them from experiencing what they really want. The focus is 100 percent on them, their story, and their results so far in this area of their life. Your job is to listen and reach common ground. Meaning that you understand their situation and where they currently are on their journey.

Ask them about their situation. Ask them how they feel about it. Sit back as they tell you their story and then simply ask them, "How has this last month been?" in regard to their pain or problem.

This question is one of the most powerful you can ask. It forces them to face the problems that brought them onto the sales call, and it puts a time constraint around it. They have to think about the pains from the last thirty days, which puts urgency on why they need to resolve them.

This is how you illuminate someone's pain.

Then you just keep asking questions. If you're really great at what you do, you'll know the patterns, the typical problems, the issues, and the things that are keeping that person up at night.

For those who I work with, it's feeling like they are on a hamster wheel, that they've made a lot of money but don't have time, that they don't have a real business.

The idea here is to be almost like a kid. Keep asking why, why, why. You have to realize that someone will have the answer rehearsed, but if you dig enough, you'll find the answer that is the inconvenient truth.

Now, my belief in this area is to start writing what they are saying. Your job here is to create an understanding of this person. The job here is to have as much presence as possible.

Most people have very few friends. They don't have many people who get them. Most often, there are less than two people in someone's life who will get them.

The most powerful thing in being able to help someone is presence—it's the act of truly listening and hearing them and allowing yourself to step inside of their shoes. Once, this happens, someone will typically take over your body.

Empathy. Empathy is powerful because it is what allows you to actually sell something. If you don't have empathy or you don't see the world through their eyes, your ability to help them becomes limited to your own perception of reality.

STEP TWO: CLEARLY VISUALIZE THE GOAL

Pain alone isn't enough to sell someone a solution. Your potential clients need to be enrolled into their vision of a better future and believe they are capable of moving through whatever is holding them back.

Now it's time to ask them to describe their goals, vision, and what motivates them. This is where they need to get honest with you about what they want. The problems they don't want to deal with anymore, the outcomes they want to see.

A key part of using this strategy is to practice active listening. At key moments, repeat what you're hearing back to your prospect. Always use their own words to describe their pain and to describe their ideal vision.

Again, you'll find that most people say what they want based on a rehearsed answer. People rarely know what will give them fulfillment and rarely know how to obtain happiness.

Your job is to understand what they actually want. Do

they want freedom? Or just more time with their wife? Do they want a multi-million-dollar business or just a hired-gun consultant?

Again, you might realize, at this stage, that this person hasn't spoken in a real way about this with anyone. Maybe not even their significant other. Further, you might find that the person you're talking to is covering their true desires and wants with those that sound cool.

STEP THREE: HIGHLIGHT THE GAP

By now, they've revealed their pain and their vision. Now, you just need to help illustrate in their mind the gap between where they are and want to be.

However, and this is important, allow them to describe this gap (instead of you stating it to them). Although you may be tempted to outright tell them what the solution is, instead ask them what they think needs to change.

A few potential questions you can ask are:

- What do you think needs to happen to change all this?
- What support would help you the most?
- What would be most valuable to you over the next ninety days?

Force them to use clear, specific language.

If you tend to work with someone over a ninety-day period (or six months, a year, etc.) ask them to share what they think they need to do during this period. Allow them to highlight their own gap because, this way, they create their own solution—meaning all you have to do is tailor your offer around their needs. The important step here is that they tell themselves what they need to do.

Most of us as humans know exactly what we need to do; however, once we say it out loud, it changes the scenario because it makes our needed transformation real. Instead of it being in our head, we are faced head-to-head with the reality that we can have it if we so choose.

Finally, repeat all this back to them once again. Ask them if they agree. Ask if you've heard them right. Each time they say yes, it creates a microcommitment that makes what comes next much easier.

At this point in the conversation, you've probably spoken for just a few moments, and they've spoken for forty-five. The important piece here is that the vibration or energy between two of you is aligned and that they've convinced themselves that they need a change in their life, business, or relationship.

STEP FOUR: CREATE A COMMITMENT

Until now, your prospects have done most of the talking. Now it's time for you to speak up. Reveal your solution as the answer to their pains and problems. This is about them and their goals; it's not about you and your program.

Say something like, "Here's how I think someone could help you achieve this over the next ninety days." This isn't about how you can help them but, rather, helping them see that this is the help they need. Once you've described this solution, ask them, "If you had this, would it be valuable to you?"

Another microcommitment. Another opportunity for them to make their own choice. Up until now, at no point has this been about you or your program or how you can help them. It's 100 percent focused on them and the help they need.

Your job is not to pitch your program; rather, your job is to be able to weave your program or offer around what they've said up to this point. This is important because an offer is more about allowing the person to feel like it's solving the problem and filling the gap than allowing for benefits or line items.

"If you don't do this, what's the cost to you?" you ask. "If you don't take action on this now, what cost will this have on you, your family, and business in the coming months?"

Asking them this brings them back to their pain and their current situation. They are desperate to change this, so the only question left to ask is: "Are you ready to commit?"

This is when you ask them whether they are ready to work with you. This is when you get specific on your offer and ask them to commit. No manipulation or scarcity tactics, none of the tricks that give sales such a bad name (and sometimes an icky feeling).

With this, the call itself provides illumination and clarity. It is in service to the potential client while also helping get them in a position to make a powerful, motivated decision to take the next step in working with you. The important part through this entire process relies on the ability for the person to come to the phone call inside of their will and with the right marketing beforehand.

When we are advising our clients, along with ourselves, we actually want to delay the amount of time someone has before they have the ability to have the opportunity to work with us. If someone is on a phone call with you and they don't know their pain or problem, they don't know your process or method, they don't know your authority, or if they don't believe in themselves, they shouldn't be on the phone with you.

The process beyond sales should be one where the person

should be validating themselves instead of validating you. When done correctly, this allows someone to look up to you, and they are pitching YOU on the sale versus the other way around.

And, regardless if they buy from you or not, they now have clarity in their life, thus causing them to make a choice. Either change it or live inside of their current reality.

OTHER MEDIUMS OF SALES

This process doesn't just work with a sales phone call.

Every single method for being able to bring someone to the point of investment or purchase relies on this same principle. It doesn't matter if it's a book, a challenge, a webinar, or a sales page. The delivery might look different:

- On a webinar, it might be a testimonial with video.
- On the phone, it might be a story about how a client had success with you.
- On a sales page, it might be the bonuses.
- On a phone call, it might be showing someone just how much value is inside and how much you typically charge.

However, the principles always stay the same throughout any way that you help someone get to the point where they say, "Yes, this feels right. I want to do this right now."

The benefit of using this method is that those who are investing aren't doing it because there's a mad dash to get it done or they feel like they should. This process reduces the number of people who will refund, it increases the number of people who will actually be able to use your services and programs, and it will result in amazing sale conversions over the phone.

It's typical for most of our clients to have 50 percent-plus close rates on the phone, allowing them the ability to not need massive sale teams, reducing their costs to operate the business.

SOCIAL SELLING 101

Most of the sales that happen for myself and a lot of my clients don't happen on a sales call or a webinar. They happen in the emails back and forth. The Facebook group, in the comments. Or the direct messages in Instagram.

You might think that someone would fill out the application or say they are ready. Yet this isn't the truth. Most people don't know they are ready to buy. Most people have imposter syndrome. Most people are afraid.

The truth is, when it comes to sales, the intimacy of conversations allows for people to feel a dopamine hit—this dopamine hit of feeling understood, or being replied to by an authority, opens the ability for a sale conversation to happen.

No, this isn't about direct messaging every person on your Facebook or cold emailing. This is about having conversations with those people who watch your Instagram Stories. It's about replying to your Facebook Comments. It's about creating the ability for connection through conversation.

Why does this lead to a sales call or an opportunity? Because you've engaged someone's attention. When someone is scrolling on their phone through ads or even reading your guide, even watching a video of yours, most of their mind is turned off.

However, Intimacy is like taking the red pill in the matrix. It's a pattern interrupt because social intelligence requires the ability to be alive. When you turn on the conscious mind, you're allowing that person to actually start thinking about what's going on in their life.

When this happens, if you've marketed yourself correctly, you're able to turn all of the marketing pieces into a Conversation that will lead to: "Why don't we jump on a call? I'd love to see if I can help you." It doesn't matter if this is you or someone on your team on your behalf. The future is about selling socially.

We crave Connection, we crave Intimacy. And those who sell socially, will come out ahead because those who feel seen and heard, spend money and take action.

HOW TO CHARGE WHAT YOU'RE WORTH

What is something worth? I mean, why is a smoothie at Erewhon in Venice Beach $23 when other places, it's $4? Why can I charge 100 times more than most others that offer the same services?

It comes down to a couple key elements that we've spoken about here. Here they are:

POSITIONING + RELEVANCY

Which one would you spend more money with? Marketing Funnel Builder or Seven-Figure Scaling Expert. Or how about Life Coach or Corporation Transition Expert.

Now, let's say you had an e-commerce business. If I added Seven-Plus Figure E-Commerce Scaling Expert or Marketing Funnel Builder. Which one?

See, the way that you position yourself is critically important. Most people don't do this because they are blinded by either scarcity (if I say what I do, people won't buy from me), or they simply don't spend enough time focusing on one thing.

Positioning is, in many ways, Relevancy, and it allows for someone to know who you are. If you say you're a funnel builder, you and 1,000,000 marketing experts are competing for the same customer. If you say you're a Seven-Plus Figure Business Expert, you're competing with 100 people. The same number of people are looking for you, yet you positioned what you do.

Further, you always control the dialogue. Our mind has a difficult time being able to remember much of anything. This is why we skim. This is why we believe fake news so easily. Our mind is looking for a shortcut. So if I tell you something, your mind will typically accept it as truth. This is powerful because the way you see yourself is the way that someone will see you.

Why do you think most entrepreneurs who have confidence or self-worth issues aren't paid as much as others? The world will see you the way you see yourself and talk about yourself. Because typically, you're the only person talking about you.

BRAND STORY

Most entrepreneurs don't truly think about their brand

story. Yet the story of your brand and what you're doing in the world is critical.

- The story of the type of people you work with.
- Why you work with them.
- What drives you to get up in the morning.
- What drives you to live the lifestyle you have.

Again, this is an element of your position. It's your job to formulate a story that allows that person to buy in to who you are. And that you are valuable.

This isn't about faking anything, it's simply about highlighting the parts of who you are in a coherent way that, again, allows the potential buyer (before they even talk to you on the phone or are on your webinar) to create a story. For example:

- Scott works with super successful entrepreneurs and influencers.
- Scott is a multimillionaire, so he must know more than me.
- Scott enjoys spending time with his wife, Libby, and thus his time is super valuable.
- Scott was in debt, and he's built a ton of successful businesses, so he gets me.

Now, all of those statements are true. However, it's also

part of my brand story. Those who want to get paid what they're worth have a brand story and talk about it over and over again, any chance they get.

NEEDING VS. WANTING

Do we want to work with the person who wants to work with us or the person who needs to? This one is simple, and it's about abundance versus scarcity Mindset. Those who are abundant and don't need us, win by default.

Now, you might be in a situation where you need it. So, what do you do?

When I was in this situation, I did abundance reprogramming, which is essentially putting your mind into a delusional space called Reality Distortion Field. This allows you to create belief systems that make your subconscious believe something that isn't true to be true. Eventually, you'll believe your own version of reality. And in my experience, it allows you to create it as a true reality.

Most entrepreneurs are good at this, as it's fueled by our inner ego-authority. This is the ability to show up and be unattached from the result. Largely, this can be done by using mantras or simply visualizing an experience as if it's already happened over and over again.

COGNITIVE BIAS

There's a lot of cognitive biases that I use in The Relevancy, Omnipresence and Intimacy Marketing & Sales Method for marketing; however, many of them have to do with the fact that when we see something (or someone) over and over, we feel closer to that brand or person.

Cognitive bias, such as I spoke about in the Omnipresence section of Marketing, allows you to charge what you're worth because, simply, you are changing the beliefs about you to someone, automatically, after they meet you online.

SOCIAL PROOF

If you've been in *Time* magazine or *Inc.*, and those are respected in your niche or industry, people are probably going to look up to you more.

Social proof is by far one of the easiest ways to be able to increase your worth. Regardless if it's testimonials or people knowing you work with certain people, again, the mind will automatically transfer authority.

You have to remember, the mind of your customer WANTS you to be an authority by default, and once you are Relevant with the right positioning, your potential customer is LOOKING for data to back up why you cost so much.

WHY PEOPLE WON'T BUY

I find it interesting that people are mystified why someone isn't investing in your offers, and I think it comes down to the fact that people believe what people say with words, not actions.

Typically, when someone says they aren't interested or aren't going to invest, they will say it's not good timing or they don't have the money or some other reason. Yet it will always come down to one of the following reasons:

1. Your offer wasn't Relevant.
2. They didn't believe in their own pain or problem.
3. They weren't your true avatar, even if they acted like it.
4. They don't believe in your method or process.
5. They don't see you as enough of an authority.
6. They didn't believe in themselves.

Inside of my business, after years of perfecting, most of the time, it's the fact that people don't believe in themselves enough. In most businesses, this is true. And it's the most difficult to overcome.

The others? Easy to fix. You can change your message, your marketing, your offer, whatever it might be. Yet how do you get someone to buy when they don't trust themselves?

This is why our marketing strategy is so important. If your

marketing is effective, it's as much about all of the other elements as it is about being able to empower your potential customers to make a choice and believe in themselves. Think about it—if someone believed in themselves, they probably wouldn't be where they are right now. If they truly trusted themselves, they probably wouldn't need your help.

I would predict less than 3 percent of society have any level of trust in themselves, which means, that a massive part of your follow-up and marketing is less about sending more case studies and more about listening for cues of not being empowered.

Now, what's the best way to bring someone over the edge of empowerment? There isn't one answer for this. However, in my experience it depends if the person who's buying is inside of an abundant Mindset or scarcity Mindset, along with how driven they are by logic or emotion.

The emotionally driven person who is fueled more by their ego will be empowered by coaching them through knowing that they have a false story and showing them it's false by calling them on their BS. This approach with a logically, non-egocentric person won't be successful; this person will purchase with a more analytical fact-based approach.

Knowing why someone says no is important. Because the truth is, "no" in sales typically doesn't mean no. It means,

"I'm not convinced in every cell of my body." And that means, you just need to become better.

IF YOU WON'T SELL TO YOUR FRIEND, YOU DON'T CARE ENOUGH

I wanted to add this part to the sales section; it's extremely important and critical.

A lot of people are afraid to sell what they have. They are afraid to talk about it. And here's the god's honest truth, if you are afraid of selling what you have, it means one of two things: either you don't believe in your product, or you don't believe in yourself.

Truly—if you don't have something you believe in—STOP, RIGHT NOW.

PEOPLE BUY WHO YOU ARE, NOT WHAT YOU SELL

Conviction and enthusiasm is addictive. I mean, REALLY addictive. We get excited when other people are excited. And it goes back to a critical part of sales and marketing.

It's the simple truth that people, most of the time, unless extremely analytical are buying WHO you are not WHAT you sell. This is true in the investment world. This is true in the dating world. This is true in nearly every element of life.

We want to buy from people that are the same as us. We want to buy from people we look up to. We want to buy from people who are successful already. We want to buy from people that really get it.

It's why our marketing is just so darn important. Because if you just rely on the sales call, you're dead in the water. Or you'll just compete to the bottom on price, features, and benefits.

WHEN YOU'RE NOT THE SALESPERSON (HIRING SOMEONE ELSE)

At the beginning of your business, a lot of the time, you will be the only salesperson. At this point, this is likely fine. However, at some stage, you're going to need a salesperson or even a sales team, and it's at this stage that most entrepreneurs get STUCK. I mean REALLY stuck.

There's a few core issues that come up for hiring salespeople. While this deserves its own book, I'll try to cover as much as possible.

The core problem around hiring salespeople comes back to the number of leads you have and how warm they are. Further, is your salesperson or team responsible for outbound or inbound leads?

Let's look at this. If you do ten sales calls a week, and

that's all the calls you have, and you currently close five of those ten people, because you're the owner and REALLY believe in your product, you've grown your business based on this.

But when you hire a salesperson, they are likely going to be 30–50 percent as good as you. That means, if you don't have MORE leads, your revenue will decrease. See the problem here? If you're used to twenty sales per month, now you're going to get eight.

Most entrepreneurs who try to scale their business by hiring a salesperson without their marketing working creates a scarcity of either cash flow, or the salesperson will leave because they aren't making enough money.

What do you do? You need to fix the marketing problem, increase the number of leads you have, and create an over-flow of leads so that you have enough wiggle room for the salesperson that you're going to hire.

The next part that is important for successfully delegating your sales to someone else is ensuring that your marketing is doing an amazing job of selling your process, method, and solution.

What I mean by this is quite simple. By making your sales-person more of an order taker versus a hard-core closer, you're able to decrease the sales cost, make sales less salesy, along with being able to increase the close rate.

One of the most powerful elements of scaling is being able to have a sales team. It's not easy at the beginning; however, if you've fixed the marketing problem, the sales problem is easy, because when you have more leads, you have more money, and that money allows you to solve the problem of sales by allowing you to have more wiggle room, especially in the first ninety days of hiring and training your salesperson.

AUTOMATION VS. INTIMACY

We've spoken about intimacy a lot; however, there's a perfect balance between automation and intimacy. Most businesses get this completely wrong. Either they overautomate their sales process, or they overintimacy, and then they can't afford to operate their business.

Automation as you grow inside of your marketing—specifically with a CRM, follow-ups, and being able to know who is likely your customer (through lead scoring, etc.)—is important.

However, don't forget this. Most of the time, someone is going to pull the trigger when you follow up. And just because someone says no, it simply means "not today." The number of people who said no on Friday but yes on Monday probably amounts to millions in sales.

The important thing when you're looking at how your automation works is to not automate the point of intimacy. That means the moment that someone attempts to talk to someone, allow them to talk to someone.

I believe that bots are great, so are autoresponders; however, they are best used when it allows for the start of intimacy with an actual human being who can help them. Business is helping humans (or, at least, it is in the year 2020) and over-automating any part of your business is going to decrease sales 100 percent of the time.

As with most things in business, I'm never going to tell you that I know everything. That isn't true. When it comes to sales, I've always used really great marketing to make it easy. I'm not the guy who can make anyone buy anything. I don't use scripts. I don't use crazy NLP. I don't overpromise.

My belief in sales is simple. Get someone to believe in the future version of themselves. Further, my belief is that if sales is salesy, it will just result in a high refund rate, a low success rate, or a business that eventually will fall apart.

If there's one lesson that *The Wolf of Wall Street* can teach you, don't sell crap, which leads me to the next most important pillar: your product.

To access the resources for this chapter, visit: www.thenucleareffect.com/resources/.

CHAPTER 6

PILLAR #3: PRODUCT

For the businesses that are currently stuck on the hamster wheel—which might be you if you're reading this book—the truth is that many of them were essentially doomed from the start.

Many entrepreneurs unintentionally design their business in a way that keeps them indefinitely stuck on the hamster wheel. Your business model and how your company's Product(s) fit within that model defines the rules of the game you are playing. And while there *are* ways to set up the game to be more in your favor, entrepreneurs often make the game *much harder on themselves* than it has to be.

There are a handful of ill-fated decisions that create broken business models and ineffective Product offerings. We're going to be going through those in this section and then show you alternative choices that can help create a thriving, stable business instead of creating an endless, exhausting exercise in hustle on your own personal hamster wheel of a business.

If we think of your business model essentially as:

- How you deliver value to the market.
- How you are compensated in return for the value delivered.

The two main pieces of your business model are:

1. How you design the offer(s) you make to the market.
2. How you design your fulfillment of the products and services you've offered (and sold).

My goal here is to share a few key lessons with you that will show you *why* so many entrepreneurs end up choosing suboptimal strategies for their business model and for their Products.

The truth is, what got you started in business, or to this point, won't get you into the next stage of the business. It simply can't. The product or service that brought you to $100K, won't bring you to $1M or to $10M. You have to pivot, you have to change, and you have to allow your model to evolve.

And most entrepreneurs attempt to scale a model, or edit their model, instead of looking at what model can actually build their dream business and work backwards. Most of the time, the model of your business that will really allow you to scale will take you years to develop, and it will require a much larger team, better operations, kick-ass marketing, and systems that make your current scenario look like child's play.

See, this is critical if you're going to scale. Because if you scale the wrong model, you won't have profit, you'll need far too much team, and even if your marketing is amazing, you might just lose more money every time you sell something, which means, the more you grow, the more anxiety you will have. Not exactly the way we want to grow a business, is it?

Let's start with *the* business model choice every entrepreneur is given.

THE TALE OF TWO BUSINESS MODELS

Many entrepreneurs start their business with a Mindset that tells them, "I'll start out by charging a relatively low amount, and then as I build up my credibility, my success stories, my confidence, and my audience, I'll start to charge higher amounts."

Unfortunately, this Mindset is a complete trap, *especially* when it comes to businesses built around coaching, consulting, training, information, transformation, etc. In the vast majority of cases, this Mindset (and business model design) will inevitably create a hamster-wheel-style business. Most businesses that take this route end up dying before they ever get to start creating and marketing the higher value offers.

And this is a pretty sneaky trap, because when you are starting at a low price, your first few sales are going to be comparatively easier. And once you get that first handful of sales, you're hooked. You're in business. And even more intoxicating, you get *that* feeling—the one where you believe you are onto something significant.

Before long though, you realize that if in order to keep making these small- to medium-sized sales, you're going to need an audience, and you're going to *need* to keep making more and more of these sales while you invest money, time, and energy toward growing your audience.

This creates a vicious cycle that becomes more and more exhausting to keep operating within. Soon enough, you find yourself totally overwhelmed and burnt out as you pour more and more energy into building your audience, while also hustling to generate new sales from the people in your audience, while also needing to give proper service to your growing client roster. In your overwhelmed state, you are going to start making some very common (and very costly) mistakes as you begin operating more and more from fear (aka from scarcity).

One of the most common mistakes is that entrepreneurs start investing in too many tools, software, and automations far too early in their business. They even implement advanced marketing before they might even know their true model or customer. They often do this because their overwhelmed brain screams out for some relief. And the allure of automated solutions plus tools calls to them like the siren's song.

The problem is that you'll find yourself shelling out more and more cash for software (not to mention for the human resources you need to help implement and manage all the tools and systems). So while you are bringing in more cash, it's going right out the door to pay the growing pile of bills, which leaves you in one of the worst places an entrepreneur can be: that place where you are always hustling to get your next sale(s) but where you don't actually keep much (if any) of the money that you're exhausting yourself to earn.

Let's compare this to the alternate choice an entrepreneur can make where they decide, "I'm going to start off charging a few people more money, or what we call High Ticket, because I know I'm good at what I do and can deliver high-value results for people. And later, once I've accumulated some cash reserves, know my process better, and have some killer testimonials, *then* I can powerfully (from a place of abundance) scale my audience and begin selling some smaller offers."

The advantages of starting with (or quickly pivoting toward) Higher Ticket Offers are overwhelming. For starters, it is much easier to have higher revenue and higher profit margins with High Ticket Offers. And because you need fewer total clients, there is less pressure to need to have an audience in order to ensure the survival of the business (like you do when you start with Lower Ticket Offers).

Not only are these High Ticket businesses often more profitable, but they are also usually more enjoyable to run for the entrepreneur. Instead of the business being an endless drain on you as you hustle on the hamster wheel only to look up after months of grinding to see you are basically in the same place you were before all that effort, your business can be a source of inspiration and motivation. Your business can provide you with true freedom and abundance. (Meaning having the resources and relationships in place to be able to access whatever you want in your life.)

And speaking of being well-resourced—when you sell High Ticket Offers, your business becomes well-resourced by your clients, which in turn allows you to better serve and take care of your clients. When their experience and their results are amazing, a couple of wonderful by-products tend to happen:

1. You'll have customers for years (if not for life).
2. Clients will be reliable referral sources.
3. They will willingly provide you with powerful, effective testimonials. (The kind of testimonials where people can just feel the excitement, gratitude, growth, etc. of your clients through their screens.)

As you profitably sell High Ticket Offers, you have the luxury of accumulating cash. Let's for a minute, take a look at the math.

LOW-TICKET MODEL
A $500 Offer

To earn $100K over the next ninety days:

- 200 clients × $500 = $100K
- 67 clients per month
- 3.3 new clients EVERY SINGLE BUSINESS DAY!
- Approximately ten sales opportunities per business day.

HIGH-TICKET MODEL
A $10,000 Offer

To earn $100K over the next ninety days:

- 10 clients × $10,0000 = $100K
- 3.3. clients per month
- Less than one new customer PER WEEK!
- Approximately one sales opportunity every two business days.

Further, think about the level of marketing that is needed for 1,000 customers versus 10 customers.

At the beginning, your marketing is going to be grassroots, it's going to be organic, relationship-driven—that's how most entrepreneurs I've helped learn to scale at the beginning, me included. Yet a lot of people that come to me think they are going to grow with a membership that costs $47 a month.

When you think of the cost of getting a new customer, churn, operations, do you really think you can get 1,000 people to buy something? And if you do, it will take another 100 per month, just to replace all the people who are going to leave.

And, let's not forget about this: Do you know that your marketing is going to convert? How much money do you have to blow on sexy marketing? Also, can you truly help those

1,000 people in a meaningful way? Or are you just thinking of the easiest thing you can do?

Having built MASSIVE memberships, courses, e-books, and everything in-between, the truth is, it takes the same amount of effort to sell something that is $100 as it does for something that is $10,000. The difference is, you don't have to sell anywhere near the same amount of people.

Now that we understand this fundamental business-model decision, let's quickly dive into *why* people buy things so that we can structure compelling offers that tap into these things.

THE FOUR REASONS WHY MONEY EXCHANGES HANDS

While there is nearly an infinite number of ways people logically justify their buying decisions, there ultimately are four reasons why people decide to give some money to someone else.

The first two are connected in that they are opposite sides of the same coin. They are both motivated from a pure financial ROI standpoint. One is to make more money, and the other is to save more money.

This is pretty straightforward. When you believe that the

additional amount of money you will earn or save moving forward is worth more than the amount you have to pay (plus any work you need to do beyond just paying some money), then you pull the trigger and make the investment.

This could be hiring an employee (or contractor or consultant or coach). This could be paying for some sort of training or course or event that will improve your skills. This could be hiring an accountant to help you save on taxes.

Basically anyone who is in the marketing, sales, or overall business niche is in some way selling "make more money" and/or "save more money." The key here is being able to illustrate a clear link between what you're offering and an improvement to people's bottom line.

The closer to the money you can get, the easier people will be able to see the value of your offer (which leads to more sales). If you can't get close enough to the money using one of these as the core driver behind your offer, this is going to be a struggle, and you'll probably need to lean more into one of the other two of these main reasons.

The third reason is to *stay out of jail*. This one is pretty straightforward as well, and the buying decision is either a proactive decision, or it is a reactive decision. Typically these are things that can help protect you, mitigate risks, and stay within the rules, regulations, and laws of your country and industry. Often these fall into categories like insurance, lawyers, accountants, compliance, and similar.

The fourth reason is the most open-ended, and it is to *have a better life*. The number of forms this can take is nearly infinite. The main categories for this are better health, better relationships, more time, recreation and entertainment, personal transformation, and powerful experiences.

"Have a better life" usually will not have a direct monetary ROI attached to it, nor will there be the kind of urgency that comes with "stay out of jail." If what you sell falls into the "have a better life" category, then you really need to be able to tap into the core pains and core desires of your market. You're going to need to be a bit more artful in your messaging to paint the picture of how much intangible value there is in what you offer.

Get curious about *why* people in the past have bought from you (and/or *why* people have bought similar types of offers from other people). Become a scientist looking for the evidence of value and get to the bottom of what makes *your* offer compelling. When you get that deep, you can take something that is a bit vague and make it clear, powerful, and persuasive.

And while there is a good chance that what you're offering hits on multiples of these four reasons, it is important to pick *one* main reason that you are going to be primarily speaking toward in your messaging and in your sales conversations. There is a *significant* difference between an offer that primarily helps you make more money (so that you can live a better life) and an offer that helps you live a better life (so that you can make more money). Once you've got your primary reason, it's time to start defining the outcome(s) that your offer is promising to people.

BE RELENTLESSLY OUTCOME-FOCUSED IN YOUR PRODUCT DESIGN

When someone is considering buying something from you for the first time, they 100 percent are evaluating it as an investment because they haven't *yet* experienced working with you, nor have they experienced the kinds of results you can deliver.

On some level, new prospects are *always* asking themselves, "Can I confidently expect to receive more value in return for the amount of money I'm being asked to pay for this offer?"

Because purchasing your service or product is an investment, it is *your* responsibility to demonstrate that there is a clear return someone will get from working with you. Your job is to show them how their life will be better by purchasing your product. One of the most valuable things you can do is to regularly take time to brainstorm how you can increase both the actual value *and* the perceived value of your offer(s).

In your marketing and your sales conversations, the Return On Investment you are offering to the market needs to be communicated clearly. Unfortunately, way too many entrepreneurs haven't thought their offer through to the point of being able to clearly state the return that their product delivers to be able to *clearly articulate the outcome(s)* people get in return for buying their offer.

Now, if your first two pillars are effective, this one doesn't have to be as good. However, if you want to unleash The Nuclear Effect, you will, without a doubt, ensure that your product is designed properly and with more thought than "Let's just do it."

QUICK EXERCISE TO CLEARLY ARTICULATE THE OUTCOME OF YOUR OFFER

Ask yourself, "What is my client's ultimate outcome?" If that is too difficult to conceptualize right now, then ask yourself, "What is keeping them up at 2:00 a.m.? What is the end result my client is trying to achieve? Could I prove in court that I delivered the agreed-upon outcome to the client?"

If the outcome you promise is something fluffy, then you

do not have a clear outcome that delivers a lot of tangible value for your potential clients. Fluffy outcomes are things like saying the client will have clarity or will feel centered or will live more fulfilled. These are the kinds of things that would not pass in court in your favor.

So I challenge you to do two things that will significantly improve the success of your offers:

1. Complete the exercise above by asking yourself those questions. Answer the questions from the perspective of the absolute best clients you've ever had (or from the perspective of your absolute, dream, ideal clients).
2. Commit to figuring out how you can deliver at least six figures' worth of value to your client in return for their investment in your offer. If you haven't already, do a realistic calculation of the value you believe your offer is worth to your potential clients. Lay it out line by line and total up the value.

Now challenge yourself to figure out how you make this number grow. (Bonus points if you can come up with ways to increase the value of the offer while adding minimal additional cost to deliver what you sold to the client.)

When it comes to the kinds of outcome your Product provides, there are two main types: vitamins and painkillers. The majority of entrepreneurs are so excited about their own Product that they can convince themselves that what they have to offer is incredibly important and urgent and necessary for the people in their market.

Remember, we *all* are firmly stuck in our own Reality Distortion Field. I've certainly been in my own Reality Distortion Field and believed that I was selling a powerful painkiller when, really, I was offering a nonessential vitamin. Far too many businesses and business models are based on something that is a vitamin instead of a painkiller.

If your business is based on something that is nice to have, it's going to be difficult. If you're simply giving an improvement and not a transformation in someone's life, business, or relationship, you will be the first thing they cut and the last thing they buy. You will have to struggle to get someone to invest in you, regardless of how famous you are, regardless of your results, and regardless of how many marketing messages you put in front of them. The harsh reality is that most entrepreneurs are selling vitamins, and those are *much* harder to sell than painkillers.

It's essential that your product or service is a painkiller. And this can be tricky because oftentimes the *real* pain your market is suffering from is not the same as the *perceived* pain they *think* they have. In order to be successful *and* remain in integrity, you will often need to sell them what they want and deliver what they need. Or sometimes people need to buy something that solves the problem they *think* they have before they can fully appreciate and understand the real problem(s) that lie underneath.

This is where you have an opportunity to provide ongoing value to people and solve a sequence of problems for them with an integrated product suite (more on this later in that section).

It is easy to fall in love with your own Product, so you need to get some outside perspectives and feedback to know whether what you've got is a painkiller or a vitamin. The faster you can get validation on this, the better. I've seen people waste months (if not years) of their lives trying to push a vitamin that they were certain was a painkiller.

And maybe you *do* have a painkiller, but perception is reality in the eyes of your market. So if they don't perceive it that way, you need to make a pivot in your messaging and/or Product structure. You either need to devise a way to demonstrate how it truly is a painkiller, OR you need to refocus the Product to address the things that your market *does* feel a level of urgency and pain around.

One of the greatest marketing lessons I've ever learned is that it is nearly impossible to create a new desire or demand within someone, but you can focus existing desires or demands onto *your* Product. Harness the power of what people *already* want, and you'll find that your Product will start to sell much easier.

If you're not sure about whether you're sitting on a vitamin or a painkiller, ask yourself this question: If you had to pitch your product in ninety seconds to your perfect customer, how excited would they be? If they wouldn't be excited, you have a lot of work to do.

Once you know you have a Product that solves a real pain for your market, it's time to think bigger picture for where your Product fits in to the overall journey your customer is on. We need to think about what other pains they have *before* and/or *after* this one is solved (and how we can be of greatest service to them throughout the process.

THE 12:12:3 CUSTOMER SUCCESS MAP

There are a few hallmarks of stable, mature business, and without this, you will continue to have to start every month at nearly zero. Quite simply a stable business is a business that has a steady line of revenue (and profit), every single month.

A few things I always look at right away when evaluating a business are:

- Monthly Recurring Revenue (MRR). How much revenue is being generated, each and every month, along with how much has a contract and how much can be canceled easily by the customer?

- Lifetime Client Value (LCV). How much revenue is being generated per customer across three, six, twelve, and twenty-four months, and what is the potential of new sales from current customers?
- Client Retention Rate (CRR). How often does a customer leave or want to leave a contract?
- Revenue Per Lead (RPL). How much revenue is generated per lead in marketing?

Very few entrepreneurs spend enough time thinking about and strategizing how their business can improve on these metrics. I promise that any time spent thinking about these things would be among the most valuable activities you can do for your business each quarter (and ideally done even more frequently). It certainly is a higher value activity than getting roped into putting out fires, getting pulled in to low-value operations within your business, or always having to be called into resolving any sticky client situations. Luckily, when you start improving those numbers above (MRR, LCV, CRR, RPL), you equip and resource your business so well that you no longer get roped, pulled, or called in those ways anymore.

It all starts with a well-thought-out customer journey and an *integrated product suite* that can help them at each of the major points along their path. Your goal here is to intentionally design your offers to match your client's journey toward *their* goal(s). When you have *clearly* mapped out what your clients' life (or business) will look like twelve weeks, twelve months, and two years after they start working with you, then you can craft offers that flow into one another. Most importantly, will help take the client fully from where they are now to where they want to be.

The truth is, most entrepreneurs don't do this. They started one on one, or a small course, or a group program. And then they needed to make more money from the same audience they have, so they launch another offer. And this is a HUGE no-no. It's normal, even typical.

Yet, if you just keep adding offers to make more money without a real plan, what you do is start creating new businesses inside of your business. This means every new offer is a new business. And if they don't integrate, now you have customers who are going to leave you. Or you haven't given enough options for the different types of customers you'll attract:

- Those who don't have enough money.
- Those who have a different learning style.
- Those who want to do it themselves.
- Those who want it done for them.

If you plan this from the start, you're able to increase the revenue of a customer and develop recurring revenue while reducing the amount of waste and operational optimization. Figure out the milestones along the way to that ultimate goal and craft ways you can get them to these milestones (including the final one).

What you will likely end up with if you do this exercise is a Core Offer, an Ascension Offer, and an Inner Circle Offer, or at least, that is one of the most effective ways to plan your business. The more you go into the future, the more offers will be created, and then it's your job to make the business come together so that you have enough momentum, enough leads, and enough resources to build an entire business that makes sense. Because that's where you'll find peak profitability and scale.

THE THREE DIFFERENT TYPES OF OFFERS
Core Offer

Your Core Offer is your initial offering, and it should have a single, clear outcome. The goal for the Core Offer is to give your client a major boost toward their ultimate goal over the course of the first twelve weeks (which is essentially a ninety-day sprint). The promise is to get them through the first major hurdle(s) on the way to the ultimate goal they want to achieve. This offer provides not just some powerful results for the client but also functions as a trial period. Here you get to decide whether the client is someone you would want to work with long term or not.

Most of the time, the true ultimate goal that people value enough to pay truly high ticket sums for takes longer than twelve weeks to fully realize. Because of that, the Core Offer flows directly into the Ascension Offer.

Depending on the nature of your business, this Core Offer could potentially help your clients afford to continue working with you on the Ascension Offer. (When your Core Offer consistency lands people in the right position where they see it as a no-brainer to keep working with you, you *know* the design for the Core Offer is on point.)

The Ascension Offer

The Ascension Offer takes the successful clients from your Core Offer and helps them achieve their much bigger goal. This is their ultimate goal—the real outcome that they are truly after. Obviously, it varies greatly depending on the goal, but for example's sake, let's say these bigger goals take approximately a year to accomplish (if they are undertaken with focus and intention).

This Ascension Offer is going to be a step-up in terms of the value promised and in terms of the commitment required from the client. (Both their financial as well as energetic commitment—remember that the depth of someone's transformation is almost always correlated to the strength of their commitment and their intention.)

Because the Core Offer is *usually* the first thing someone buys from you, potential clients are considering the Core Offer as a new investment. But when they are considering the Ascension Offer, they have already received value from you well beyond the price they paid for the Core Offer. Beyond that, they've now been regularly paying you for a few months, which means that paying you has now been normalized a bit. When you provide enough value, clients start seeing you as a regular normal expense that is a key part of their growing success in business and/or in life.

The Ascension Offer is the key source of regular, recurring revenue for your business.

Being able to make individual sales that then pay you monthly for a whole year will give you completely new levels of freedom and security in your business. When you have a solid Ascension Offer in place and you've built MRR that is greater than your monthly expenses, you're able to have peace of mind in knowing that each and every month's expenses are essentially guaranteed to be covered. It means you can actually take a break from the business every once in a while without worrying about what will happen if you don't hustle your way into creating multiple new clients over the coming weeks.

With Monthly Recurring Revenue, the days of starting over from zero dollars each month are over. That money is coming in regardless of whether you do any new marketing and sales efforts or not.

The Inner Circle Offer

The Inner Circle Offer is an *unadvertised*, highly Intimate program for a very few, select clients. Clients at this level typically have an exclusive level of access to you, and this usually includes at least one or two private days or small group Mastermind events.

Your Core Offer and the Ascension Offer should be *designed to scale*. But the Inner Circle Offer is *designed to be limited and exclusive and intimate*.

The Inner Circle Offer comes with a significant investment and is reserved only for people who *you* would be thrilled to spend that much time and energy with (whether you were getting paid for it or not). And while it *is* incumbent on you to deliver a lot of value to these high value clients, often a huge part of the value people get from Inner Circle Offers are from the community of amazing people in your Inner Circle and from the greater depth of relationship they get to have with you.

Honestly, this offer is likely going to stretch you. It's going to force you to discover new, powerful ways to deliver value to clients. As an additional benefit, you can often take these new discoveries from this offer that stretches you and leverage them to positively impact *all* of your offers. And one more advantage is that your Inner Circle Offer will often create some of your best partnership opportunities, licensees, and referral sources.

I want you to realize that this doesn't always work. Depending on your marketing, depending on your audience size, depending on your business goals, it will change.

If you have a million followers, I might suggest a membership. If you have $10 million in the bank and want to scale, I might suggest a $197 product.

Business is a game of a lot of ifs; however, in my experience, 80 percent of those I work with will have success with the above. Simply put, if you want growth, you need cash. However, if you want sustainability, you need monthly recurring revenue. And if you want to scale your audience and marketing, your leads need to pay for themselves.

INTIMACY > PERFECTION

I think most of the time, entrepreneurs fail when they try to be perfect. Or they wait to launch until it feels like the right time. Simply put, if you feel good putting something out, you waited too long.

While you are taking on a serious responsibility by offering a *very* high ticket offer, you are better served by being real, open, honest, and vulnerable with the people in the program than you are trying to be perfect. When you try to be perfect, you set yourself up to fail. Maybe you can keep the facade of perfection up for a while, but eventually, we all slip up. And if you've presented yourself or your program as perfect, then there will be broken expectations.

If you instead allow a greater level of connection and sharing of your true self, then even your mistakes can be turned into powerful, valuable areas of growth, insight, and opportunity for both you and for your clients.

Later in your business, you'll be able to add the other elements you may see online, things such as a membership, a course, or a Mastermind. And you'll be able to make it look sexy and have automation; it'll be world-class. But, in the beginning, if you don't just get it out, and add YOU, then you may never scale.

HOW TO REMOVE YOURSELF FROM PRODUCT DELIVERY

In the life of every entrepreneur, there comes a time where a major issue comes up if they want to scale: "How can I trust someone else to deliver my service or product? There's no way it will be as good, and people won't buy it because it's not me."

I'm sorry to tell you, the chances are, as an entrepreneur, you aren't the best person to help your customers. Your ability to articulate problems, create methods, be creative and be the leader—is amazing. Being the coach or the mentor or the person recording content or anything in between. You probably weren't created for that. Someone else was. And that person likely isn't an entrepreneur, doesn't want to be, but rather, wants to help YOUR customers using YOUR method and process that is inside of your head.

The ability to remove yourself from delivery comes in two parts. The first is the Mindset, which we just spoke about. The second is the literal hiring of someone else.

Now, chances are, if you have an online business, there are people following you today that are looking for something extra. They also would likely love to work with you. And at the point when you know you can't scale any longer, it's time to bring in support to help with your programs, products, and services.

However, before this, you have to develop a method or process that allows for that person to deliver the exact (if not better) experience you give each and every one of your customers. Once you have this done (which we cover in this book), it allows you to train your team to deliver a world-class experience which systematically delivers the intended outcome that every customer has when they invest in your solution.

Now, here's the more important point. Once you do this, your ability to scale and your ability to actually have scale is unleashed. If you work in your business, you can work forty hours per week. If you have a ten-member team, it's the same as you working 400 hours per week. A forty-person team? 1600 hours per week. That means in a week and a half, they will have done more work than you could do in an entire year. That's scale—and it requires YOU being out of the delivery of your business.

Or you don't have a business; you just have a team supporting your one-on-one work.

When you design your Products so that they're all about your client, their goals, and their journey, you set your business up for massive success. The best companies in the world are customer-focused, and you can join them by designing your offers to deliver powerful, ongoing results (or value or transformation) to your clients.

Now that you have a bulletproof product design strategy, all that's left to do is to relentlessly and effectively execute on that strategy. Which brings us to the Fourth Pillar of an online business—Operations and Team.

To access the resources for this chapter, visit: www.thenucleareffect.com/resources/.

CHAPTER 7

PILLAR #4: OPERATIONS AND TEAM

You can't scale a profitable business by yourself or, at least, not a very big one. I remember a mentor of mine asking me, "Scott, do you think you can get to where you want to go *all by yourself*?" See, being able to operate a business, a team, and client delivery is a completely different set of skills, and most entrepreneurs aren't that great at it by default.

If you don't have a team, it probably seems scary. If you have a team, it's probably scary thinking about scaling it even more. Further, if you want to be a multimillionaire, and you aren't going to have a team, it's going to take a long time or you're at the top 0.001 percent of the population that are able to do that.

Think about this: if you have a team of ten people, you technically can get 400 hours of work done per week. That's a lot. However, because entrepreneurs aren't typically great at managing people, systems, operations, or processes, this section in the book is going to cover the easiest way I've found how to do it.

The truth is, one of the most important parts of operations for an entrepreneur is having a massive respect for it and allowing yourself to hire people who can manage the outcome of what you desire. Most businesses fail because of their operations, team, culture, or client delivery because the entrepreneur didn't invest the resources or allowed the team to do their job, and the business comes crashing down.

I made tons of mistakes when building teams and managing people. In the process, I discovered a lot and also realized that I'm probably not the best CEO out there. Most of the stories make me embarrassed. From not giving my teams enough time off, or creating a toxic culture, while I'm an extremely nice person, the problem with managing a team is that you're managing emotions.

In marketing, this is easy, but in business, managing a team is all about managing emotions for being able to fulfill your vision. And regardless of what we want, there's no version of us being able to build the company we want or fulfilling our vision without other people being brought into your vision. There's only so far a team of VA's that are underpaid are going to take you.

It takes true buy-in to your vision for real success and a business that will grow beyond you. The important thing is that you make continuous growth and progress toward building a powerful, effective team around you. It doesn't just happen one day that your ideal team is built: a team that actually takes most of the work *off* your plate that empowers you to work more often in your zone(s) of genius and to step more fully into a true leadership role. This is the kind of team that truly helps you grow a sustainable, profitable business.

It is a journey to—over time—attract, retain, develop, and empower great people for your team with multiple key milestones along the way. And to best understand *who* your team needs most is to start by understanding YOUR role in the business.

THE THREE ROLES AN ENTREPRENEUR CAN PLAY IN THEIR BUSINESS

Understand that there are three primary roles you can take within your business, and while you likely have some skills and experience in several of them, we all naturally fit best into one of the three. The three personalities are the starter, the operator, and the scaler.

A starter is someone who's really good at sourcing ideas and implementing the best ones with speed and momentum. Many entrepreneurs are starters. They're good at quickly deploying new things, getting traction quickly, and building MVPs to validate their ideas. Typically, they're naturally talented at marketing and sales (with the ability to generate momentum FAST).

In my experience, this is the case for most entrepreneurs; generally they are AMAZING entrepreneurs but not an amazing business owner or CEO. They are good at manifesting a vision; for many of them, it feels like they are downloading from a super consciousness or from their very creative self. And once they put it on paper or spend a little time making it happen, they are ready to move on to the next phase.

An operator is someone who can steadily operate a business that's already gotten traction. They're enormously talented at finding and fixing the problems that plague businesses as they navigate growth. They're incredible at identifying processes, systematizing things, and making the operations of the business smooth and seamless.

Lastly, a scaler is a unique personality. These entrepreneurs have a special skillset that allows them to take an existing business that's operating well and grow it exponentially. While a starter can typically get a business from zero to the six-figure range (and sometimes to the seven-figure level), they often get stuck there. A scaler's specialty is taking a business that's already successful and multiplying on that success. A good scaler will help you begin generating unprecedented year-over-year growth in both revenue and profit.

It's important that you know which one of these you are. Because if you're a starter, you *need* someone else to be your operator. And likely also a third person to be the scaler. (Personally, I'm an amazing starter.)

Whenever you build a business, remember an operator and a scaler are extremely important or the business will max out at around under $5 million. And honestly, if you don't have an operator at $1M, you're at massive risk, which is typically where you need an operator or scaler, or the business will fail.

Knowing your role is *critical* for understanding exactly what you should be DOING with your time and energy for the business because it'll allow you to know the right people to hire. If you're an operator, it's probably best to have a co-founder or hire a CMO to help you build the needed momentum and traction. If you're a starter, you'll need a good operator or COO (managing as a CEO, typically) in order to grow. If you're a scaler, you're actually probably not an entrepreneur, or you're an entrepreneur that is a veteran. I see very few entrepreneurs who are true scalers; these people typically are already running eight- or nine-figure businesses.

Right now, it is a near guarantee that you are doing way more than you should be.

HOW TO GET THE MOST IMPACT FROM THE HOURS YOU DEDICATE TO YOUR BUSINESS

If you're like most entrepreneurs, you probably think that you're the most important person on your team for your business's continued growth and success. Even if you're humble, then certainly at least in the top two or three most important. And even the *most* humble entrepreneurs likely are holding onto at least several tasks that they can actually let go of: the fear tells you that no one else could do *this* task as well as you, and you may be right.

It is 100 percent possible that no one else will care nearly as much as you do. Or that no one else in the world sees the full picture of the business the way you do. And it definitely will require spending some time to train others when transitioning responsibilities, tasks, and outcomes to them. But even being right about those things, that Mindset won't help you grow.

In order to grow, you need to be able to let go and to delegate. The first step is understanding exactly what you're doing right now on a day-to-day basis. Only after you are clear on where your time and energy is going can you start effectively delegating to elevate yourself to your zone of genius—doing the things that create the most value for others and for your business.

To do this, it's really simple. Go into your past week and write down every single thing you've done. If you can't remember, at the end of the day for the next week or two, write down every single thing. Taking the time to do this audit is *key* because entrepreneurs are typically terrible at estimating how much they're doing every single day.

Once you have a clear view into exactly what you're doing, begin separating out the $10 per hour tasks from the $1,000 per hour tasks that truly only you can do in your business.

Now, the first time you look at this audit, you may feel a sense of being overwhelmed, or perhaps you won't know what to do next. The main fear usually is along the lines of, "If I'm not doing all this, who is going to do it? And what am I going to do with my time now?" This fear is ultimately tied to something very critical when it comes to giving yourself the freedom to really grow your business. And it's the fear of not knowing who you are if you're no longer doing all these things that you've convinced yourself you have to do.

What you need to remember is that *you are not your business*. You and your business are separate entities with entirely separate goals. And while a lot of the goals can overlap, there are plenty of important differences and distinctions.

If you're currently a solopreneur, you need to *prepare yourself for a shift in identity*. You have to get used to being interdependent with others—**trusting and empowering them to help you** build the business. Being completely independent and operating without your team's help is a recipe for frustration for everyone (ultimately pushing valuable team members away in the process).

A proper business is a *system* that delivers value. It's a machine that churns out revenue and profit month after month. Your business isn't you. You are not your business. If you build a business around you, you don't have a business, you have a team of assistants. A business is a business; once you exit, it still operates, builds profit, and grows. That's it. Period.

In order to get your business consistently producing value separate from you, you need a team. You aren't the business. The business is your team and your operations (aka systems).

I've failed at this so many times because most of us want

to feel important, and most of us want to ensure that we are needed and wanted. It's sort of like this: we want to feel needed but not be needed. But in order to not be needed, you have to build a business that works without you. Yet that brings up a lot of insecurities.

- What if the business fails?
- What if it doesn't work?
- What if a team member leaves me?
- What if someone steals from me or takes my clients?

The list goes on. And I can't promise that these things won't happen. However, are you going to live in fear, or are you going to empower your team and give them an environment that would make it silly for them to do anything else?

So you may be asking, *"How can I build an amazing team that can take my business and grow it into a profitable machine?"*

THE SECRET WEAPON TO BUILDING AN INCREDIBLE, EFFICIENT TEAM

The best, most profitable companies in the world have mastered the art of making their businesses places where their team wants to be. A strong culture is key for powerfully enrolling team members into your business. This means that *everyone* takes ownership of the mission and the vision of the company.

Your team will work harder and go beyond the call of duty for your business (and your clients) when they are working on something they love and believe in. When your company becomes a destination for high-quality talent, you will have no trouble hiring and retaining amazing people.

Yet this is one of the most difficult things to do and is one of the most difficult elements of being an entrepreneur. By the time you figure out your values, your mission, and your vision, it's probably changed.

And here's where the lesson that you aren't your business, is important. When your business has its own identity, its own values, mission and vision, it allows for it to be part of you but not be you.

As you build a business, you are going to have a persona evolution that separates you further and further from what you do inside of the business. However, if YOU are the business, that means that your team is really only going to ever be able to work with you because it pays them well or they find it cool or they feel obligated to help you.

At around the million-dollar-per-year mark, it becomes

critically important for you to start collaborating with your team on building your vision, your mission, and values.

MOST ENTREPRENEURS WON'T DO THIS

They find it boring, they aren't inspired by it, or sometimes it feels like it's even an imposter syndrome.

Think about it this way. You have a business, a child of yours—it might feel like. And now, your job is to define how that business acts. How it treats its customers, its team members, and everything it does. Your job as an entrepreneur is to birth this child and allow it to be who it wants to be in the world, separate from your own identity.

This is a process, and while you may want to go and generate more revenue, launch a new product, or do whatever the entrepreneur mind might want to do, it's extremely important that you have a level of respect and honor for what you will create. It will allow you to attract talent, it will allow you to have a certain magnetization toward the marketplace, and great culture allows you to build a business with a strong foundation that doesn't require you.

So how does this work? There's plenty of books on this; however, first I start with the following:

1. What change do I want to see in the world, that my business can change?
2. What does that change look like?
3. What values are important so we get there and that we would be willing to fire our best team member, if violated, or fire our biggest customer if they violated them.

You can make it far more complex; however, once you and your team have developed this, it becomes the cultural fabric. It now allows for the people on your team to have a clear direction and outcome. It allows for your customers to know that they belong (or don't). It allows for others a definition for what you do.

And the best part? In time, it becomes the reputation of the company that you founded. Instead of just you. See, as an entrepreneur, the business you have today is likely not the one you'll have in the future.

You'll birth many kiddos (aka businesses), and if you ever want the ability to step away or sell the business, this is a critical element. Because the day you make the mission not making you rich but, rather, building a better place to live on the planet, you'll automatically get wealthy in the process.

Those who provide massive value to the planet get massive value in return because, in my experience, the world and the universe works in a balanced field. Everything will always equal out.

HOW TO HIRE THE RIGHT TEAM AND WHEN TO DO IT

There are a lot of factors that go into hiring the right people for your business. And while a distinct, powerful company culture is the most important element, it won't do you any good if you don't continue to value and protect that culture.

Bringing even a few bad culture fits onto your team can kill morale and can create some very expensive issues in your business. Remember that when it comes to hiring the right person for your business. Their character, personality, and work ethic are far more important than their current ability to do the job.

Competency in the position you hire for is obviously important, and the cost of admission to even be considered, but if it's a choice between someone who is less experienced but a perfect culture fit versus someone who is a poor culture fit but a bit more seasoned in their craft, long term, your business will be better off if you hire the person who is a good culture fit and then train them to become exceptionally good at their role.

The power of a strong culture is that your team members

will stay with you longer, work harder, and champion your company far more than a normal team member would for a company with a mediocre culture. Essentially, there is a tremendous invisible ROI that comes with having a strong culture.

In summary: Hire for fit. Train for skills.

HIRE WHEN IT HURTS?

You may have heard it said that you should only hire when it hurts. In other words, bringing on new team members when you are at your breaking point, where you simply can't keep moving forward without bringing on someone to help handle the growth.

And it's true to a certain extent. Early in your business, you usually don't have a choice but to hire when it hurts. And when you're growing fast, you typically have periods of time where the resources to hire another person simply aren't there. In those cases, you and your team have to carry the weight until you're actually able to hire someone (with the confidence that you'll continue to be able to afford to keep them on board moving forward).

Your job as the entrepreneur is to decide where you are in your growth versus profit cycle and then:

1. Create consistency and have confidence in your ongoing lead flow and sales so you can anticipate your hire because now you have a level of predictability in the growth.
2. Commit to hiring when it hurts if you don't have confidence in your ability to sustain your lead generation and sales. If you hire when you're unsure if you can actually keep team members on board, you'll actually end up with a huge hit to your bottom line, and you may have to let go of the people you just hired. Letting team members go hurts morale and company culture much more than having your existing team hustle a little harder for a short amount of time.

Most of the time, entrepreneurs get this wrong. They either hire far too late or far too early. What you have to realize is that it typically takes ninety days for someone on your team to actually become fully productive, and it takes a lot of training in order to get someone to the point where they are actually productive.

So what do entrepreneurs do? When things are feeling good, they hire. When things aren't, they don't hire or, worse, fire.

This comes down to entrepreneurs actually having a plan, actually knowing what business they are building, and realizing that their financials should decide their future hiring. Not their gut.

HOW TO GUARANTEE YOUR TEAM HELPS (INSTEAD OF HURTS)

Unfortunately, there are plenty of entrepreneurs who have built a team around them only to find themselves *still* stuck on some version of the hamster wheel. Most of them have fallen into the very common trap of creating a team environment and dynamic where the team is totally dependent on the entrepreneur in order to get anything done. And that is a recipe for making your quality of life worse, not better.

As an entrepreneur, you're likely a visionary. You can see what you want so clearly that it can be difficult to remember that other people don't see it the way you do.

To illustrate what I mean, if I say to one of my team members, "Hey, I need a stove," they could spend the next five hours rummaging around for firewood, gathering supplies, setting up a fire, and creating a wood-burning stove. But what my team thinks I mean by stove may be completely different from what I mean by stove. They couldn't have known that I wanted an electric stove unless we sat down together to discuss it and reached an agreement on what we *really* want to build here (in a way that allows for effective execution as soon as the decisions and agreements are made) and if the thing you want to build is going to be a regularly occurring item, then you (or, even better, someone on your team) need to turn it into an SOP (Standard

Operating Procedure) if you want to be able to get a regular, duplicatable result every time this need comes up.

Unfortunately, most entrepreneurs suck at creating SOPs. We'd rather eat eggplant raw than sit down to document and create a process. When hiring a team, *it is their job to create the SOPs* and to clearly define the tasks. Hire people who can do that for you.

Your job is to give direction and to provide clarity. Your team figures it out and then comes back to you with what they've built. *Empower your team to own outcomes, not just tasks. That* is a key part of creating a team and company culture that leverages you to do your best work in your zone of genius.

For years, and years, I've done this. It's a skill that I'm still working on, and it comes down to communicating exactly what you want in clear terms. And this isn't just about you; it's about your team member. Remember, what we say isn't always what the other person might hear.

In my experience and my advisory for entrepreneurs, it's important that you hire an operator in your business early who can translate what you say into what you mean. In my companies that have been successful at execution, this has been critical. Why? Well, the operator's job is to take your vision and translate it to the rest of the team as you grow, and if you think that you can translate it, you'll typically be wrong.

Now, what happens when you don't do this? More than likely:

- You will be misunderstood.
- The wrong things will happen.
- You won't get what you want.
- You're going to want to fire your team.

Because you'll just say *I'll do it myself.*

THE 10/80/10 RULE

A rule that has been extremely important in my life when it comes to building a business has been the 10/80/10 rule.

When you hire someone, it's exciting and scary, and then you have the *oh shit* moment: "How do I get you to do something?" Here's what's worked for me.

At the beginning, work with them to understand what you want and how it should look, helping them articulate everything—this is the first 10 percent. Then let them go on it, the 80 percent. After they come back, you add the last 10 percent, and you have 100 percent.

Now, at the beginning, the percentage may change. It might be 10 percent/70 percent/10 percent/10 percent or some other version. However, the importance here is that you stay involved while allowing them not to be micromanaged.

You don't need minions; you need people who can run your business. There's a difference, and micromanaging creates minions, not leaders. Your job is to create leaders.

As my good friend Gerard Adams says in his show, "Leaders create Leaders."

AUTOMATION AND TECHNOLOGY

I could write an entire book on automation and technology, but I'm going to keep this short and sweet.

At the beginning, don't worry about having the right automations and technology. People spend SO much time getting things right. And the truth is you may never get it all right. There is always going to be more in your business that you can automate and always a new piece of software.

In my experience, the more automation, the more your business is stable; however, at the beginning, you need to be able to innovate and break things quickly. That means your technology doesn't have to be perfect.

People obsess around the wrong things; just let it go. Pick something. You can always change later. And you will if you grow because that's just how business goes.

TASK VS. PROJECT VS. OUTCOME HIRING

There are three different types of people that you can hire inside of your business. Most entrepreneurs don't know the difference, and because of this, they have a completely different expectation, and then the reality isn't that great for them.

- Task: People who you hire for tasks, you are telling them to do something, you're giving them a specifically designed task that takes someone to do it (and is not automated), and they are accomplishing that task and then moving onto the next task. For example: publish a new blog post on my website using our Standard Operating Procedure.
- Project: This person is managing or completing an entire project, so this might be developing a marketing funnel or implementing The Relevancy, Omnipresence and Intimacy Marketing & Sales Method, designing or developing landing pages, emails, and getting something done that goes beyond a task.
- Outcome: This person is actively creating a result, for example, giving the person the outcome of producing 10,000 qualified leads a month.

Now, do you see how this works? If you get a task person, they may help you get 10,000 leads, but they may just be the person who is reviewing the ad copy. If you get a project person, they aren't concerned or responsible for the 10,000 leads.

Most businesses are bottom-heavy and have too many task-based team members because they are far more affordable than project or outcome roles. However, who is going to get something done better? The person who is outcome-based, project-based, or task-based?

The more ownership someone has over what they are doing and the more connected to the outcome, the better the result for you as an entrepreneur.

THE MINDSET OF YOUR TEAM VS. YOUR MINDSET

If you're a team member or an employee, your Mindset is incredibly different than if you are the owner of the company or the founder. And here's the issue, dear entrepreneur. Your Mindset is never going to be the same as those who you hire. It's not their job. This is going to bug you a lot.

You're going to say, "Why don't they pay attention to detail? Why don't they care like I do?" Or your team members might amplify small problems and make them big.

Here's the deal. If the people who worked with you were like you, you wouldn't be able to hire them. So you have to do a very important thing if you want someone to have the founder or entrepreneur Mindset versus the "I show up and get paid" Mindset. Enroll them into the vision and mission of what you do.

Now, here's the truth. If you don't have one, your team will always look for a new opportunity. If you don't have one, people will be showing up, and they can only be as good as their natural character.

In my experience, if you want to scale past a few million a year and you want your team to have the founder Mindset instead of the employee Mindset, it's critical that you actually have something that they can buy in to from a mission and vision perspective. Further, from what I've seen, this is even more effective than giving them a percent of upside on either profit or equity. Those who stake their existence on a mission will typically be successful.

But what do you do if you don't have a big mission right now in your business? The easiest way to work with this is understanding the mission of the individuals of your business and then aligning your business with their mission.

Someone's motivation is rarely about money; it's about their mission and vision for their own life. If you show someone how they are going to get closer to that on an individual basis, you will keep your people for a long time.

INTERNAL COMMUNICATION

One of the largest challenges with a business is being able to communicate as a team. While I've had in-person teams along with virtual teams, being able to communicate properly is important.

A very important part of having culture, is being able to communicate and being able to have time when not everyone is working. I know, that sounds counterproductive, and for entrepreneurs you might be thinking, "I'm paying to allow people to connect?"

Yes, you are. Connection, as you've discovered, creates Intimacy. Intimacy is needed for a team to be able to work effectively. If your team is virtual, a lot of this is done through having time for people to connect with each other.

At my past companies, I've done things such as group meditations, fifteen-minute hangouts, connection roulette, team retreats, coaching calls, and personal development.

If you look at someone like Chip Wilson, the founder of Lululemon, you'll see that he requires everyone to complete a six-month personal development program for all team members. What you have to realize is that communication entirely, both on a business and a personal level, is extremely important as you build a culture.

On a practical level, I believe in management software such as Wrike or Asana for being able to manage team members and projects with your team. I also believe in the simplicity and fast response of a program like Slack, which allows for messaging outside of email, and then a product such as Zoom for video and audio communication.

I see so many entrepreneurs that build businesses complicate the process of communication as they build their business. One of the core issues that I see is that once you go past about a dozen team members, your communication will start naturally breaking down unless you create a process for effective communication and have platforms that everyone knows how to use.

Business in many ways is like most things in life. Communication. And team communication and connection is important if you want your business to run smoothly.

THE BUCK STOPS WITH YOU

When you start building a business, or when you are in any level of leadership, you are responsible for whatever the team does, regardless if you knew it happened or not.

This can become stressful and is a huge reason why a lot of entrepreneurs decide not to scale a business, because the responsibility and energetics becomes increasingly difficult if you don't have great practices. This also means that as you build a business and as problems occur, you're going to need to be the one who simply takes the blame.

One time, over ten years ago, I had a marketing agency. One of our team members ordered $39,000 worth of print material for a client with a critical spelling mistake on the cover. Yes, it was his fault; however, it was also my fault, and I had to take the blame (and paid the bill for the reprint).

Another time, we sent an email out to 122,000 people that had the completely wrong timing. The single email created over 1,500 unsubscribers along with a lot of semi-pissed-off keyboard warriors.

Another time, a bill didn't get paid, and it got into collections because of a miscommunication issue with the person who paid my bills.

I've had so many team members. I've hired and fired hundreds of people in my business. These things are going to happen. It doesn't matter how good you are or how good your team is.

HUMANS, NOT ROBOTS

If our business was run completely by robots, you could say that things would be simple. Yet that's not how it's run. It was built by a team of people, and a team isn't really that easy to always manage. Further, every single person that you hire has their own life. They have their own trauma, experiences, and stresses in life.

For example, if someone isn't paid enough and they need to have a second job and are always tired. Or if they are drowning in debt. Or if they just had a kid. Or have a video game addiction. Or whatever it might be. How do you think they are going to show up?

Now, I'm not telling you that what's going on in the lives of your team members is your responsibility; it isn't. However, the illusion that your team members are going to just show up, forget about their life, and work with you with the highest level of productivity isn't going to happen.

This means the better you are able to take care of your team—the more flexibility, the more time off, the better you pay them—the better they can perform. Now, there's a lot of nuance to this. There's a difference between being taken advantage of and giving someone a life where they can be productive.

However, when you hire someone, you don't just hire their

skill or ability to execute. Just like dating someone, you date all parts of them. Good, bad, or ugly. Which means, it's your responsibility to help your team as much as you can. Not doing this means low productivity, and when you do this with your team, they will further connect to you, become loyal, and become loyal to your vision and mission.

SOPS

Standard Operating Procedures. I would truly rather do almost anything besides write one of these. And you're likely like me. The good part? You don't have to write them; your team does.

However, having SOPs in your business is CRITICAL for success. Without a way to know exactly how something is done, guess what happens? It'll be done one way on Tuesday, a different way on Thursday. Quality assurance? It'll never happen.

Most entrepreneurs feel overwhelmed with this. However, as you build your business, you have the ability to shift your responsibility to your team to develop these critical documents. As they complete tasks, as they build out new products or services, they are able to document their work. This allows them to achieve a higher status and promotion in your business while also protecting you if they leave or are sick or gone from the business.

The major issue with a lot of entrepreneurs is that they don't build this into their culture, and when this occurs, they don't get created. Imagine having a business of fifteen team members, and there's no internal documentation. This makes it so there is no checklist. There's no way for someone to take a day off.

Essentially, the more you scale a business without SOPs, the worse client delivery you're going to be able to have.

When you want to blow it up. At some point in your time of managing the operations of your business, you're likely going to have moments where you want to burn it all down. There are going to be times where the team messed up. There are going to be times when a client didn't get what they needed or were promised. There are going to be times when you have to outright fire your best team member.

Quite simply, running a business from an operational standpoint has a certain level of stress, and you're going to end up fantasizing about an earlier time when things were easier: when you didn't have a team. When you didn't have structure. When you didn't have operations.

And I'll be honest, I've been there before, and I've even blown up those businesses. And I don't have any good advice beyond what you likely already know. Which comes down to a few key elements.

1. In a moment of something occurring, it feels much bigger than it actually is. In a year from now, will it matter?

2. As entrepreneurs, we guard our reputation, which means when someone messes up, we feel like we failed or that it comes back on our character. The truth is, it does. However, the good news is that, typically, it's a limited issue, and transparency and honesty is always the best policy.

3. Respond; don't react. Take time to breathe, meditate, and NEVER react to ANYONE, ever. Things always get worse.

4. Always have gratitude.

5. Your memory is typically fairly terrible and reminding you what life used to be like; thus, it will trick you into potentially going backward.

6. At every stage of growth, it's painful; there's a reason why most people don't do it.

The simple truth is: if you don't have an operator in your business or if you don't hire a CEO, it's likely that you WILL blow up your business. Because trying to turn yourself into an operator is out of integrity with who you are as a human being.

If you're an entrepreneur, you're a natural creative. If you're an operator, you're a natural system creator. Know who you are and double-down on it. You were put on the planet for a reason.

At times, it can feel like interviewing, hiring, training, and managing a team is a drain on your time and energy (not to mention taking on increased risk and liability). And at times, it can feel like creating processes and operations is getting in the way of doing the actual, urgent work that needs to be done for clients. These two statements are especially true if you identify as a starter as opposed to an operator or scaler.

But you and I both know the truth, and the truth is that if your business is going to be able to grow and thrive over the coming years, *a solid team is absolutely necessary.* So even if it sometimes feels like focusing on *this* pillar is slowing you down, remember this: if you want to go fast, go alone. If you want to go far, go together.

Just remember, building a great team is a process, and one worth committing yourself to, because if you want to have a business that gives you freedom (meaning you can go do what you want, when you want, for whatever reason you want), an effective team is critical. And truthfully, a lot of mistakes made around operations and team happen because of flawed financial management and/or a flawed Mindset.

Luckily, the last two pillars are Finances and Mindset, so let's move on to Pillar #5.

To access the resources for this chapter, visit: www. thenucleareffect.com/resources/.

CHAPTER 8

PILLAR #5: FINANCES

The fact that I'm allowed to talk about finances is some-what ironic to me. When I was a million dollars in debt, I never thought I'd be giving people financial advice. I guess, regardless if you do something good or bad, you still learn. I've lost millions of dollars. I feel like I've made nearly every mistake you can when it comes to managing your money and being able to manage your finances as an entrepreneur.

As you grow your business, you will have to regularly nav-igate some key financial decisions. Unfortunately, even smart entrepreneurs get these key decisions wrong an alarmingly high percentage of the time. Most entrepreneurs are in a complete place of delusion or reality distortion around their finances. Mostly, this is because of the fact that they are extreme optimists. This is a double-edged sword because, in my experience, entrepreneurs don't make great investment choices; they make big bets.

One time, when I was on a cruise ship about six years ago, I started with $100 in a casino. Now, this was the first time and one of the last when I gambled. However, two days later, I was up to $20,000. I was playing roulette. Call it luck, or the way that cruise ship was moving. But I was on fire.

Why? Because I took the same bets I made in my business. I remember this one critical point where I said, "I'm done. I just lost $4,000 on a single spin."

It brought back my feeling of losing everything. I ended up cashing out and not coming back, even though they invited me back for free.

I tell you this story because most entrepreneurs treat their business like a casino. Most entrepreneurs are delusional. Because you are smart in one thing doesn't mean you will be smart in another. Most entrepreneurs invest not knowing enough data. Or they go in debt to grow instead of going into debt to invest.

While I don't believe that more money = more problems, it is undeniably true that more money = different problems. Unless you are lucky enough to have gotten some advice from someone who has already made these new, different decisions before, it's easy to fall into a handful of traps that end up significantly harming the Finance Pillar of your business.

There are three main reasons why these financial mistakes are so common for entrepreneurs:

1. Because proper financial management is rarely taught (and certainly not covered in our schools).
2. Because our culture, community, and family have given us bad programming around money and how to *actually* use it to create growth and momentum.
3. Because when we are as invested in something, as we are with our business(es), we have a *lot* of emotion attached to it.

It is easy to let short-term emotions drive significant long-term decision-making (which almost never ends well).

I certainly made these mistakes while running my first couple of businesses (several of which, despite my errors, were still able to grow to the multi-seven-figure level). Actually, I discovered most of what I know about finance, when the stakes were BIG and the problem is at that level, it's hard to course correct. Creating a new Mindset of financial understanding when you don't make a lot makes for a much better future.

My hope is that this section will let you learn from the various mistakes I've made as well as share with you the best financial advice I've been fortunate enough to receive so far on my entrepreneurial journey. Let's start with the bare minimum things you *need* to know about your finances as an entrepreneur.

WHEN TO HOLD, WHEN TO FOLD

Most entrepreneurs don't know when to make bets on themselves and when to let go of something. In my experience, here's how to know:

- When to invest: When you have a high level of confidence that the outcome will allow for a level of return on investment within a time period that you're comfortable with.
- When not to invest: To sustain something because you're invested. This is loss aversion, the number one reason why people lose everything and the reason why I went $1 million in debt.
- When to invest: When you know that you need to get the momentum going and are spending money on training, mentorship, or knowledge that will cost ten times more if you learned differently.
- When not to invest: When you are protecting your ego or attempting to look like you're not failing even if you are (aka losing money).

- When to invest: When you know that it's not an all-in bet and that you can recover if it doesn't work, or you can offset the bet by taking other actions.
- When not to invest: When your gut tells you that it's the wrong choice.
- When to invest: When you know your financials and numbers and know exactly what the next ninety days look like if you don't make another dollar.
- When not to invest: When you are on an emotional high, or you just got a big payday.

Simply put, your ability to make good choices comes down to your numbers (logic), your ability to bet on yourself (ego), and the level of short- or long-term return on investment that you're looking for.

THE CORE FINANCIALS ENTREPRENEURS *NEED* TO KNOW

Especially in the first couple years of running their business(es), entrepreneurs are susceptible to letting their emotions make their business decisions for them. And if entrepreneurship wasn't hard enough already, it's these kinds of emotionally driven decisions that make the whole thing excruciating. (Honestly, I really wouldn't recommend trying it to any sane person.) But because you are crazy and ambitious enough to go for it, I hope this section makes a meaningful impact on how you operate the Finance Pillar of your business.

Choosing to run a business means choosing to *regularly* put yourself into high-pressure positions where you have to make difficult decisions. And through regular exposure to all this pressure, you're either going to grow and become better through it all, or it's going to break you (and almost certainly taking your business down in the process). It's enough to simply reiterate that business owners often let short-term emotions dictate their financial decisions.

Here is what that emotional decision process looks like:

1. Look at how much money is in the bank account.
2. Look at how much money is coming into the business during the next thirty days.
3. Make a *decision based on how you feel in the moment* after looking at number one and number two above.

Whenever you make a decision using this (or a similar) process, you are *always* reacting to the whim of temporary circumstances instead of leading your business toward your ultimate vision for it, along with what your business can afford versus what it cannot. It's the difference between having *intentional* financial management where your decisions are made to continually build toward the vision you hold most deeply for your business versus doing that emotional decision process where you'll make erratic decisions based on temporary circumstances instead of making clear, powerful, intentional decisions.

I've been here so many times. And guess what? This process is exactly like so many of those cognitive biases you've already heard of. Even after you are fully aware of what this emotional bank balance financial management looks and feels like, you can *still **easily*** fall back into running your business this way.

For example, in my past, for a company I owned, payroll went out early in the month each month. And after $250,000+ leaves my business's bank account, I am feeling *way* less open to adding another expense compared to how I feel in the days later in the month when the business gets multiple $50,000+ payments at the same time—this wasn't smart behavior.

The hard reality is that if you make choices based mainly on your bank account, you'll crush yourself. You'll either spend money too loosely when the account is healthy, or you'll find yourself unprepared for opportunities because you don't have the proper resources to take advantage when they arise. The main concern here *isn't* necessarily whether a particular expense is a good investment or not. Instead, the bigger concern is the fact that we would make a different choice solely based on what part of the month the opportunity came up in.

I know for a fact that I've passed up on investments that would have gotten me to my goals much faster but instead made an emotional decision based in fear and scarcity. Further, I've invested in things I shouldn't have because I had the illusion I had more money than I had because I wasn't truly looking at my financials.

You see, it is easy to get swept up in an emotion and to make decisions from a triggered place. And it is considerably harder in an emotionally charged moment to consciously choose to recenter, to refocus on your ultimate goal, and to make a decision *only* after taking a more objective, long-term look at your business.

THE NUMBER ONE MOST IMPORTANT THING ON YOUR FINANCES IS THIS

Do **NOT** stick your head in the sand when it comes to the hard numbers of your business. They are easy to avoid, but it will cost you greatly if you do (potentially even costing you the whole business). Even if you feel embarrassed about the current state of your business's finances (or how much attention you've been giving them), here's the truth: the only person judging you, is you.

Business is a game measured with dollars and cents, so looking at your finances can be a difficult, uncomfortable mirror to look into. But being brave (and being real) about looking at what is going on is what is going to allow you to make the best possible decisions for your business.

If you are going to pivot toward making solid, long-term financial decisions, there are only a couple *absolute must-have* pieces to your finance plan. If you haven't been on top of your numbers lately, there are two critical first steps to take.

The first is to be proactive in regard to taxes. One of the largest expense items for profitable businesses are the taxes they pay, but many entrepreneurs find themselves being reactive to their tax bill instead of having solid projections and a disciplined plan for putting away money to match the projections. If you get behind on taxes, it can become a difficult ditch to dig yourself out of as the government charges a healthy interest rate on back taxes (not to mention they can add a whole bunch of stress and misery to your life as well).

The second is to make a commitment to begin tracking your cash flow *now*. We want to project out for thirty days and ninety days from now. This includes how much revenue is coming in over the next thirty days and ninety days, expenses over the next thirty and ninety days, and liabilities over the next thirty and ninety days. From these numbers you can calculate your estimated profit over the next thirty and ninety days.

You don't need to build a perfect financial dashboard or tracking sheet right away, but you do need to have insight into your major numbers and your cash flow on a regular, ongoing basis if you are going to make the right choices for your business. Further, smart management of your business comes down to looking at your financials on a weekly basis and making your choices not based on your bank account.

The entrepreneurs I know that are successful never look at their bank balance. Rather, they look at their P/L and liabilities. This allows them to properly make choices that are based in reality instead of reality distortion.

Your bank balance will lie to you. Your ability to know all your expenses, all of your liabilities, and all of your revenue doesn't lie. Your profitability doesn't lie to you. You can justify in a moment based on your bank balance. You can't justify with emotion looking at all of the numbers. There's no such thing as just doing it. You are doing it with calculation.

And the truth is: this isn't fun. However, business is a game of numbers. And if you don't treat it that way and respect it, you'll end up on the wrong side of luck.

Now that you have the foundation for a stable base, let's explore one of the most common finance mistakes entrepreneurs make due to emotional decision-making. And that is making the choice between whether they're going to operate in Growth Mode or in Profit Mode.

GROWTH MODE VS. PROFIT MODE

Growth costs money; it sucks money. Here's the truth. When I grow a company quickly, I don't profit a whole lot. If I'm being brutally honest, most businesses I've grown, I've grown way too quickly. Mostly, this was due to my ego, and because of this, it taught me how to grow while doing it in a sustainable and responsible way. However, it wasn't always like that.

I've grown businesses faster than someone that took ten years. That's not because I was better, I was more willing to invest the money back into the business. You will need to regularly make decisions to balance between Growth and Profit. If you want to grow quickly, then you will have to move quickly. And moving fast opens you up to greater risk of making mistakes that cost you money (not to mention the increased investments you need to make into a marketing, team, and operations when *choosing* to be in Growth Mode).

If you want to shift to Profit Mode, you'll move much slower. Profit ratio will increase, but your rate of growth will slow down. Ideally, you're using this time to stockpile some cash that can be used for a larger investment or to make the right investment at the right time. In some ways, Profit Mode is biding your time a bit while in search of the right opportunity to return to Growth Mode.

So the questions you have to regularly ask yourself are:

1. Is now a time for profit or for growth in my business?
2. Based on where I believe my business, my market, and the economy as a whole are going, do I believe we will be able to *earn greater profit later* in this business by choosing to grow now?

Before you answer those questions, there are a few things to consider.

With Growth Mode, you are plowing your revenue back into the business to fuel its continued growth. You are sacrificing greater profit now to drive yourself toward greater profitability in the future. You are going to likely make some uncomfortable investments when you are in Growth Mode. You will also likely test yourself and your team a bit as you attempt to do new things (and work fast) while trying to maximize your growth.

With Profit Mode, you may find that it actually demands more of your time personally. And that is usually for one of two reasons.

For businesses under the $50,000 per month mark, it is usually because you have fewer people on your team (whether they are employees, contractors, or coaches/consultants) when you are in a Profit Mode. And that means that there will be more things that you have to own.

For businesses over seven figures, it is usually because entrepreneurs who have made it to this level are more driven by vision, mission, and growth than they are by money. And without the excitement of being in Growth Mode, they find ways to insert themselves more and more into the business to try and give themselves and get the high we can get from our businesses.

Typically, when I find entrepreneurs who are fueled by growth, it's typically (not always) fueled by their own ego, and they want to prove something to themselves or others. Why do I know that? It was me for years and years.

Most of the time, there is a happy medium, where you can grow AND profit. However, growth is addictive. Because growth feels like momentum. And momentum is addictive. And it's the drug of choice of entrepreneurs because entrepreneurs are at many times in their life ego-driven.

Also, one of the first expenses entrepreneurs tend to reduce (or completely cut) when they switch from Growth Mode to Profit Mode is their marketing and lead generation budget. When there is no automated way of generating new leads, it is often the entrepreneur who is responsible for generating new business when other lead sources have gone away.

Neither mode is better than the other. It is simply about what your business needs right now and you being aware of the pitfalls of each mode in advance so you can avoid them.

You also have to truly look at your life, I mean, the life outside of your business. What's important for you? If you have no kids and no other person to take care of in your life, and you really believe in your business and yourself, maybe you want to push your luck. However, there comes a time in every entrepreneur's life where there is a balance, when it can't be about beating last year's revenue and it's more about profit or lifestyle design.

See, there's no wrong model. We all have our own beliefs and ideas for what we want our life to look like. I've had times where I bet it all (and lost big). And I've had times where I bet it all (and won big). Today, I don't bet big, because, I left the casino.

Now, here's an illusion. Most entrepreneurs do not create wealth through their direct business. Most of the time entrepreneurs who I mentor get their business to the point where they can either sell it (or part of it), they can take the cash flow and invest it, or they make their money in external opportunities (which is why audience and relationships are so important).

In all honesty, the only time I see multigenerational wealth created by entrepreneurs, it's like this, which is why you can't grow profit and have wealth all at the same time. It's different, and based on where you are, you make choices differently.

You can't go from a $500,000 per year business to $2 million per year and profit $1.5 million easily (might actually be impossible). However, if you run a $2 million per year business for five years, you'll build wealth. Or if you build it to $10 million and then sell it, you'll have the money for your wealth.

That's why this book is focused on building your business. Because in the build phase, you'll probably still feel broke. It's important you decide where you are and stick to it. The Nuclear Effect can unleash in your business, and if you aren't ready, it will break your business because you'll grow past your comfort zone.

THE FOUR DIFFERENT TYPES OF CASH

One of the key parts of being smart with your Finance decisions is understanding the different types of cash there are in your business. The unfortunate truth of business is that you aren't going to actually collect all of the cash that your business generates.

Pretty much *every* entrepreneur can tell you a horror story or two about how they made a sale, agreed to a contract with the client, and then ultimately weren't able to collect some (or any) of the money the client agreed to pay. Whether the client experienced something catastrophic that crippled *their* cash flow and had to ask to be released from the contract, or the client completely ghosted while still owing thousands of dollars never to be heard from again, or if legal action had to be considered (which is its own drain on your money, time, and energy), the risks are real.

I've had so many times where what I thought would happen, didn't. One time, I had a client walk out on a contract that made it so I lost a couple million dollars in billings—it made me have to pivot an entire part of my business.

Planning *your* finances based off assuming you're going to collect all the owed cash that hasn't been collected yet is playing with fire.

There are the four types of cash in your business:

1. **Cash Generated.** This is the total contract value of your agreements with clients.
2. **Cash Collected.** This is the total amount of money that has been successfully received from your clients.
3. **Cash Outstanding** (aka Cash Liability). This is the difference between (1) and (2) above. Let's say you sell a client on your Ascension Offer, in which the agreement

is that they're going to pay you $5,000 per month for a year. And let's say that so far, they've made payments for the first three months. In this case, your Cash Generated is $60,000, your Cash Collected is $15,000, and your Cash Outstanding is $45,000.

4. **Cash Liability** (aka Accounts Receivable) is *not* guaranteed to get collected.

The business graveyard is filled with companies that increased their spending too fast based solely off of Cash Generated that hadn't yet been collected and then, for various reasons, experienced one of those horror stories in which they were never able to actually collect the cash. As a result, the company was put in a significant bind, or worse, the company folded completely.

A lot of the time, the issue isn't about *if* the cash can be collected but, rather, *when* the cash can be collected. Even slight misalignments from when you *expect* to collect cash and when you *actually* collect it can lead to significant consequences. At minimum, it can strain relationships with your employees or vendors when your major expenses have to get paid, but you're waiting on delayed incoming cash before you can pay.

If you've ever been burned before by a client who you ultimately weren't able to collect from, you know how it can cause you to feel a lot of stress, fear, and create uncertainty around the rest of your current Cash Outstanding. And it can be hard to let go of those negative feelings.

As mentioned in the Product Pillar, one of the best things you can do to soothe negative feelings and restore confidence is to build your Monthly Recurring Revenue (MRR). Because you have known recurring collected revenue each month, you take out a lot of your risk. You become less susceptible to unexpected issues, like an inability to collect from a client.

The ideal scenario is to build your MRR to the point where it covers your expenses each month (aka your burn rate). You'll be amazed at how freeing and empowering it is to know your business's expenses are paid for each month. Having that can powerfully lift you out of scarcity and allow you to start pursuing the opportunities you've been talking about—as you wait for your business to be more stable before going after them.

Without MRR, your business is fully dependent on being able to make new sales each month to generate more cash and be able to collect all of that cash. You will almost certainly experience boom/bust, feast/famine cycles, where sometimes you are fighting to make what you need to keep operating the business.

The choice is yours whether you will begin thinking and

acting toward how to grow MRR in your business. Overall, these four types of cash need to be properly managed, and you need to be thinking in terms of revenue collected, not earned.

One more piece, before we move on. One thing I see that stops a lot of entrepreneurs in their tracks is liabilities of delivery that they didn't have in consideration: this means someone bought for six months in advance but on month two requested a refund. Refunds have collapsed entire businesses.

While I don't believe in the negativity of thinking of the worst thing, I believe it's important to keep track of the liabilities of what money you've collected that you haven't actually earned. And remember, when it comes to contracts, a lot of the time, unless it's to do with a lot of money, it's not worth the paper it's printed on.

Plan for the worst; manifest the best.

HOW TO *REALLY* THINK ABOUT SPENDING MONEY AND MAKING FINANCIAL DECISIONS

Most people are fixated on the short term and driven by the fear that they won't have enough money at some point in the future. Because of that, they are always focused on what needs to be done *now* to ensure they have enough for the upcoming period of time.

A surprising number of entrepreneurs live in scarcity mode all the time and find themselves hustling day after day because they need to hit certain revenue levels each month in order to keep the lights on. But if your plan is to be in business for a long time (whether with this particular business and/or with future ones), then you can't be continuously stuck in the short term. It's an unsustainable strategy.

If you can spend more time with your focus on the long run and if you can consistently choose to play the long game, you can direct your money toward things that grow and appreciate over time. You can find more things that create exponential growth, accelerate momentum, and unlock The Nuclear Effect in your business.

Further, a trap that I've found myself in time and time again in my business was "just enough" syndrome. Essentially, each month I would attempt to generate just enough money to cover expenses and pay myself instead of actually profiting.

A lot of the time, this is due to the Mindset of actually profiting or thinking it's dirty when, truly, it isn't. If you don't have a profitable business, you have a really expensive hobby. And a business isn't created to break even. It's created to profit, so you can create a great life for you and your family.

Even if you don't care about money, or even if you don't think that it matters:

- Do it for the time you might get sick.
- Do it for the next venture you want to create.
- Do it for your unborn children.
- Do it for your future lover.
- Do it for the future version of you that needs the tens of millions of dollars in the bank to take care of your parents in their old age.

At some point, you won't have the wellness to hustle like you're used to. Make the money while you can, even if it's not something you value.

PART OF THE ART OF BUSINESS IS KNOWING WHEN THERE ARE EXCEPTIONS TO RULES

When you're growing a business, there are times when you may have to do things in the short term that might not be in alignment with your long-term strategy in order to generate some cash.

We're all open to many different potential business risks (as well as personal risks) and sometimes things happen. Sometimes we have to do some things that hurt in the short term for us to be able to put together what is needed to actually be able to build toward your long-term strategy and vision.

THE SUCCESS TRAP

What's the first thing that happens when an entrepreneur starts to really have success in their business? A lot of the time, they go out and upgrade their lifestyle.

One of the entrepreneurs I mentored that didn't take my advice went out after a launch that was super successful and upgraded their car to a Tesla, started eating completely differently, and moved into a new house that cost five times more than their former. Guess what happened? They stepped into the success trap.

This happened when I was younger. I got used to living a certain way, and because of it? Now, I had to generate a certain amount of money to just maintain my lifestyle.

This is also the most difficult one to avoid. You hustle for year after year. You see everyone else living an amazing life. And you're stuck in the same apartment, spending the same amount of money.

So what's the rule for lifestyle? For me, it comes down to passive or recurring revenue. I do not take more money out of the business than I can afford on long-term recurring revenue, or as many talk about: passive income.

The worst thing you can do as an entrepreneur is have a taste of success but not be able to eat the entire thing.

The other thing about upgrading your lifestyle, it's really critical as entrepreneurs that we can have as much money in the bank as possible so that we feel safe and secure so we can make good choices. The more scarcity you have, the worse choices you make. The worse choices you make, the more you're robbing from your future.

This trap also happens because a lot of entrepreneurs show off their success. And this is where the ego will come in and slap you in the face or punch you outright at times.

The thought is: "I said I made X dollars this month. I didn't, but now I need to keep up appearances." Or, "If I have X, more people will buy from me."

Now, I'm not going to lie, this might be reality. However, if your business relies on keeping up appearances, at some point in the future, it will all come crumbling down. And that extra money you make from keeping up will just go into your lifestyle.

See, most entrepreneurs, and people in general, will scale their lifestyle along with their business. When this occurs, you actually don't make any more money. You just have a nicer, comfier hamster wheel.

The whole lifestyle design movement, in my mind, is around this. I'm not telling you that you can't have a great life; however, don't scale it as fast as you're scaling your business. Stay one or two steps behind your business and allow time for accumulated revenue (aka profit) to then pay you. It'll be hard to do this, as it takes a lot of willpower. However, if you set these boundaries, you'll never fall into the success trap and have to make money just for show or, worse, for your overpriced car and house.

MANAGING DEBT, INVESTMENTS, AND SAVINGS AS AN ENTREPRENEUR

What I'm about to write is not advice I would give a typical person that isn't an entrepreneur. In general, you'll likely never see this advice anywhere. It comes from a billionaire that mentored me when I was a teenager, and it's proven to work extremely well for me and those who I've mentored.

As I've said, I ended up a million dollars in debt. I paid back every cent, with interest. Keep in mind, this debt wasn't good debt or property/asset debt. This was credit cards, lines of credit, friends, family, and suppliers. That probably makes me an expert on how to get entrepreneurs out of debt.

Further, I've invested millions of dollars into myself, my audience, my education, and mentors. One of my mentors, over the years, I've paid over $350,000. It's worth every single dollar.

So let's talk about debt, investments, and savings as an entrepreneur. What you need to understand about entrepreneurship is to manage finances since it doesn't work for you like it does for any other human being, and most financial advisors will never be able to help you.

See, most conventional jobs are based on a linear growth model. That means you start at $48,000 per year, then $55,000 per year, and twenty years later, you might make $112,000 per year. All while saving as much as possible to put in savings and retirement.

Entrepreneurs are different. Entrepreneurs are based on exponential growth curves. That means you can make $40,000 per year for five years, then $2.5 million the next year, and then sell the business for $20 million. And thus, this gives me beliefs on the following.

INVESTMENTS

Until you are in wealth mode and you have a high level of profit that you are going to use in investments, the best investment you can make is the investment of yourself. That means hiring mentors, bettering your knowledge, having wellness, and reinvesting inside of your business.

This means that not a lot of your profit should be reinvested outside of your business until your business is stable and able to generate dividends and while your business has matured. Remember, your business has a specific time in the market. If it's your time, then invest and invest heavily. Once you know it's time to get out, sell, dilute, or pivot.

However, the chance that investing in someone else is going to have a higher ROI is extremely low; betting on yourself is critical.

DEBT

Most debt is extremely cheap and—outside of debt that is tied to someone else that is your family, or for taxes, such as the IRS—has a smaller interest rate than your potential level of growth. For example, my lines of credit were the very last thing I ever paid off because it didn't make any sense. If your interest rate is lower than your ability to have profitable growth, it's better to reinvest that money instead of paying off the debt.

Let's do a little math. Let's say you have $50,000 of debt, and the interest rate is 20 percent. That means that it costs $10,000 per year to have that money. With $50,000, can you make more than $10,000? That's a question for you. For me, it was yes.

Now, here's where it is tricky. Debt has a lot of stigma, shame, and guilt. Further, because of your parents and society, it likely causes a lot of stress. Thus, most of the time when I have someone pay off their debt, it's not because they needed to pay off their debt. It's because it stays on their mind and puts them into a scarcity Mindset.

Debt, when used properly is an amazing way to have extremely high growth without having to spend that money yourself. It's only when you go too far, or beyond your means on a business that isn't working, that it is problematic. Meaning, you go $250,000 in debt without seeing any traction in your business.

Bet on yourself, but check your reality distortion at the door, and don't get wrapped up in your own dream.

SAVINGS

I think savings are smart. However, if you have too much, more than likely, it's more about your Mindset than it's about needing it.

The general rule is to save enough money to live your personal life for six months and for your business to have four months of cash in the bank. Now, keep in mind, this depends on your growth mode, where you are in the business, and what you're looking to do.

One of my mentors, who ran a public company always had

four years of cash in the bank, and he truly believed that it gave him the advantage, as he saw that new opportunities at that level took a lot of money. For me, I've yet to get a non-consulting company at that level of financial stability, and it takes a long time being in business to be at that level.

However, keep this in mind, the only reason for savings is largely to keep your Mindset at peace, and it does very little for anything besides that. However, don't discount that. Your ability to be in an abundant Mindset is what allows you to make the best choices in your business, so find your benchmark and guard it with everything you can.

Now, these strategies and beliefs are mine. We all have them, but know this: most of the beliefs you have around money came from your parents and your experiences up until this point in life.

HOW TO PAY YOURSELF AND TAKE MONEY OUT OF THE BUSINESS

One of the core problems that I see with many entrepreneurs is that they use their business bank account as their piggy bank. There's two core problems with this.

PROBLEM ONE
If you do not pay yourself a fixed monthly salary (or at least

a fixed amount of money you say you're going to), you'll find yourself just spending money, you'll look at how much money is in your bank account, and you'll just find things to spend money on. I've found very few entrepreneurs where this isn't the case, and it's extremely dangerous because your bank account isn't an accurate representation of how much money you have available.

PROBLEM TWO

If you don't overspend, but you don't pay yourself, you're going to see your profit margin, and it's going to be far bigger. Further, if you're underpaying yourself, meaning not paying the market rate, you're going to underestimate how much money you actually have and are profiting (or paying taxes on).

For example, if you're making $50,000 per month, but only paying yourself $5,000 per month, then your profit margin might look good, but in reality, the market rate for you might be ten dollars, or even $15,000.

For growth, this creates an issue, and you should be paying yourself (or at least saving this for paying yourself) so you can grow with an accurate profit margin. Don't use your bank account as your piggy bank. I'm not telling you not to write things off, or pay extra in taxes. Just monitor and budget because if you don't, you will spend all your money in ways you'd rather not.

HIRING OUTSIDE HELP

When I was younger, I went to an accountant. They were really good, and they spoke about their fees. I didn't value what they did. If I had hired them and sacrificed some money, I would have saved millions of dollars later in my life.

In my experience, you need three core people on your team when it comes to your finances, and if you don't have them, at some point, you'll be screwed.

A bookkeeper. Most businesses have no idea of their finances. They do bookkeeping once a year, and that's it. This needs to be done monthly, and weekly, once you're making over a million dollars a year.

An accountant. Not one that is just preparing tax returns; one that is going to be able to actually tell you what's going on and what's happening, preparing you for your taxes and giving you a level of insight of what's happening.

A financial advisor. I'm not talking about the personal one that is going to get you to invest in 401(k)s. I'm talking about a business financial advisor. This is someone with a lot of experience who is going to advise you of the future of your business.

Think about it this way:

- The bookkeeper is in the back seat of your car, telling you what happened.
- The accountant is in the passenger seat, telling you what's happening now.
- The financial advisor is in the car a mile ahead, telling you what to expect and how to plan.

This doesn't cost that much, and I can tell you, this will make you profit far more, spend less in taxes, and allow you to sleep at night. It took me ten-plus years to get to this point, and it was a game changer.

MARGINS

As we discussed in the Product Pillar, it is actually *easier* to deliver a high ticket program than it is to deliver a lower ticket product. And that is because you have *significantly* better margins when you have a well-designed Product. Better margins mean you have the resources to hire better people, who are *also* equipped with better tools, resources, and processes to take care of the delivery *for you*. In fact, it is a near certainty that there are people out there who could do as good a job teaching or implementing as you would (and possibly even be able to do it *better* than you can).

Margins mean you can reclaim your time and energy. They are how you get leverage on yourself. They are a key piece of building a sustainably *profitable* business. Getting leverage on yourself means that you, the entrepreneur, actually get to work fewer hours (while also paying yourself a bit more from the fatter margins).

Back when I was hustling to do nearly everything in my business, I never thought this could be a reality while also earning the kind of income I wanted. But with the right high ticket offer(s), it can be.

We recently had a six-figure initial launch of a new product that requires less than five hours per month of my time to create and now to fulfill. Even with our $100,000 offer, I spend less than four hours per week in any element of it. It is run and delivered by my very capable team, who I'm only able to afford because our clients give us the resources needed to retain this hypertalented team.

Obviously, this takes a little time to build to this, but I remember spending YEARS dreaming of being able to work twenty hours PER week while operating various services, consulting, and agency businesses. The path to that starts with improving your margins.

The truth is, your business is a game of numbers, and I know that doesn't sound like much fun. More likely, you're an entrepreneur a lot like me. We love cool ideas, concepts, and solving problems. However, the ability for you to impact the world and to have a business that really makes a change in the world relies on you being able to actually have profit so that you can do what you say you're going to do. Most entrepreneurs that I meet don't have a love for money, because if they did, they likely wouldn't be entrepreneurs; they'd be investors or true business owners.

However, if you don't have an appreciation and respect for the numbers as an entrepreneur, you're always going to come up short. That vision that you have, will never happen. The ability to protect and provide for yourself and your family will be limited, and someday, you won't be able to make money the way you're making it now. The economy will change. You won't want to do it. You won't have the health. You'll want to do something else.

Further, as I've said earlier, there's a day when your true purpose will reveal itself, and in this time, you'll want to be prepared. Part of this preparation is being financially independent and wealthy, being able to take the energy that you've collected in the form of money and transferring it into the reason you're on this planet.

People might look at "profit" like it's a dirty word, but it's a beautiful element of allowing us creators to create, move mountains, and change the world.

I'm passionate about money; the reason is I've messed up so much. I could write an entire book on financials, and no one would read it because no one wants to talk about it. No one wants to make the choices that are hard, and most entrepreneurs aren't willing to put their logic hat on and really dive into their financials and take responsibility.

Instead we take their drug, which we call momentum, and we grow beyond our means, and we build a company that everyone else congratulates us for. Yes, we stay rich on paper and poor on money.

There's a reality for you to have both. You just have to decide you're going to do it.

To access the resources for this chapter, visit: www.thenucleareffect.com/resources/.

CHAPTER 9

PILLAR #6: MINDSET

There is a very valuable by-product that you get whenever you improve in any of the previous five Pillars. When you increase your competency in your Marketing, your Sales, your Product, your Operations, or your Finances, you *automatically* improve your Mindset as well.

INCREASED COMPETENCY = INCREASED CONFIDENCE

Making progress and seeing increased results can provide both temporary as well as permanent boosts to your momentum and upgrades in your Mindset. Because Mindset is so intimately tied into all the other Pillars, I like to call it the Omnipresent Pillar because it's the number one thing that will create success or failure in a business.

An entrepreneur's number one downfall is themselves. And the ability to have success comes down to seeing how an entrepreneur sees the world or a set of challenges. A challenge and an opportunity are the same; they're just seen differently. Anxiety and excitement are the same emotion. As a friend of mine, Tucker Max, says, "It's just felt and perceived differently."

In this final Pillar section, we will go over how to strengthen your Mindset so that you can powerfully handle *any* obstacle and show you how to graciously accept (and then build upon) your well-deserved #wins without falling into complacency or self-sabotage.

The truth is this: your Mindset will create your outcome. It will decide what you do, how you think, and you can typically see the success or failure of a business based directly upon their Mindset. Think about it this way: the Mindset, values, and beliefs that you have today have brought you to where you are. They've been formulated from your friends, parents, books, and those who you follow and surround yourself with.

Most entrepreneurs who succeed are those who are open to change, and they see their beliefs as theory, not law. Inside of business, those who see what they believe as laws typically fail.

Because the world changes and what we must do to be successful will change every single day. Further, as we evolve, we upgrade our consciousness as we upgrade our ability to be aware of ourselves, our emotions, our reactions, and our whole selves, the more we're able to understand what's stopping us from the next level.

Most of the time, those entrepreneurs I work with don't have an actual pillar problem as I talk about in this book. Everything I talk about can be found online, by both me and many other business experts.

See, most of the people I work with need mentorship, coaching, and therapy of their Mindset in order to upgrade their Mindset. Because it's their Mindset that stops them. Because most of us know exactly what we need to do, but we're just afraid of that next level inside of our Mindset and limiting beliefs.

If we solve this and build a process for your Mindset while allowing you to know that you're normal, we unleash the ability for you to actually implement what's in this book and all the pillars in your business so that it's not just a hustle; it's a true machine that delivers value to your customers.

LET'S START WITH YOUR MINDSET AROUND YOUR BUSINESS

One of the biggest things that stops entrepreneurs from

maximizing their success is not **thinking big** enough about their business. For one, the goals they make are often too small. And after being in the game for a while, entrepreneurs tend to become less bold and less audacious. They become programmed by people in their industry and begin blindly accepting the limitations of those other people. This herd mentality is a big reason why most people get average results. (And in business, the *average* result is FAILING within five years.)

You need to set higher goals. You need to raise your expectations for your business (and for what your business can create for *you*). The truth is that if you have a BIG vision for what you and your business can create, if you want to make the greatest impact you can in this one lifetime of yours, then you *need* a business that is at the seven-figure level or beyond.

If you want to create the kind of impact you *want* to have in this lifetime, you will need to earn healthy profits to fuel the efforts. You need cash, connections, and an audience to make a more significant impact. And a scalable, profitable business is the best way to grow how much you have of those three currencies. Without a *highly* profitable business, it will be a struggle to fully actualize your fullest purpose and create the most meaningful impact you can for those you serve.

Think about it this way: if you don't feel safe and certain

in your life, if you don't make enough money every month automatically to pay for your life, and you have years of money in the bank in case something happens, if you don't have things taken care of for you and your family, then the chances of being able to actually serve the world at the highest potential are low.

Why? Because our highest level of service is when we don't expect nor need what comes in return.

When we help someone else, it's an exchange of energy. When the exchange of energy isn't needed but, rather, comes back to keep balance, it results in a high level of profit. This allows you to make long-term choices. It allows you to operate all pillars with clarity while ensuring that you're doing what's the best for your customers and your industry instead of what's best for your bank account.

Without a *thriving* business, you will simply keep running around on the hamster wheel (feeding and reinforcing a scarcity-based Mindset with each step). I know that you aren't building up your business (and your Mindset) to *just* make money or have a luxurious lifestyle. Or maybe you are, for now. Yet having had all those things, fulfillment doesn't last for long.

In my case it took only three days of having my Dream Supercar before I realized, "Maybe, this wasn't it."

Of course the lifestyle is nice, as are the things and experiences success gives you access to, but if you're going to generate the energy needed to reach that level of success, you usually have to be fueled by the freedom, fulfillment, and happiness that *only* come while on the path of your own personal *why*.

And what I'm about to share is an incredibly powerful reframe around your why and your purpose.

HOW DO I FIND MY PURPOSE?

First off, it's totally okay if you have no idea what your purpose is right now. (And if you believe that you currently *do* know your purpose, well, there is *always* more that can be revealed to you about it.)

I believe our purpose is revealed to us over the course of our lives through what is called *emergence*. Similar to how the entire blueprint of a perfect oak tree is contained within a single acorn, the highest expression of your self exists within you (and always has). But if the mighty oak is going to grow from the acorn, it requires the right conditions to emerge. It needs to be planted in fertile soil, get plenty of water and sunlight, and not fall prey to natural disasters or to human or animal intervention of its growth.

If you are going to emerge into knowing and living your

purpose, you need the right conditions too. The first thing you need to know about these right conditions is that it is impossible to truly know yourself when you're constantly stressing over the day-to-day concerns. You need to be able to take some longer-term perspective to see more of the full picture, and that is extremely difficult when these kinds of questions are always buzzing somewhere in the back of your mind:

- How am I going to pay these bills?
- Is there enough money coming in this month?
- Am I charging enough? Why am I working so hard for *this?*

It requires a real commitment of time and energy to connect deeply with yourself, and so long as you're worrying about where the next client is going to come from, you will never be able to fully unleash your *why* into the world. The constant nagging of questions like the ones above make it hard to reach the levels of peace, serenity, and freedom needed to figure out what *your* next best steps are.

"Freedom" is defined as when you are able to look at your life and can confidently say, "I am able to do what I want, when I want, with who I want to do it with. And I am able to do so simply because I want to."

Having access to *all* the people, places, things, and experiences you most desire, without any of the emotional hang-ups around your worth or worries of whether you deserve the things you want or having the nagging feeling that you're an imposter (or maybe even an asshole) for having it sounds like freedom to me.

And here's the truth: if you aren't happy at $100,000, you won't be happy a $1 million or more. And while having a profitable, seven-plus-figure business has been a driving force in helping me to have more time, freedom, fun, and fulfillment than at any other point in my life, and while my business allows me to truly do what I want in life (which is to feel completely free within myself as well as making a bigger impact for others), I learned how to *start* finding peace and happiness when I was still climbing my way out of debt.

The best version of you is NOT connected to money. But money *can* accelerate you toward your best self, as you can free up more time and energy while also investing toward the experiences, knowledge, and mentoring that can help your emergence. Your best self will begin to emerge faster and faster when you no longer need to dedicate so much of your time and energy to keep your hamster wheel running, where you're hustling and hustling and hustling but never *really* getting ahead. Having a real business that creates value and generates profit (even if you barely showed up) can provide you with true freedom and abundance.

Strengthening each of the Pillars shared in this book can help you create a powerful business. And if you want to have a big impact, a seven-plus-figure business isn't nice to have; it's a necessity.

Even if you aren't currently clear on your purpose, you can begin preparing yourself *now*. You can begin to equip and resource yourself will cash, a team, an audience, and relationships. That way, when you do find your purpose (or rather when it finds you), you are ready to move forward with massive momentum.

My hope is that this book will be instrumental for you as you build a business that can fuel your purpose in life. To help you further on that path toward seven-plus figures, I want to share with you...

THE MINDSET OF A MILLIONAIRE

When I meet entrepreneurs who are earning six figures, they tend to already know most of the tactics, strategies, and information they need to be able to scale to seven figures (and beyond). And thanks to the internet, *everyone* has equal access to the information they need to succeed.

The biggest obstacle is almost always that the entrepreneur gets in his or her own way. It is *always* your thoughts, beliefs, and Mindsets that keep you stuck playing a smaller game.

But the best thing about the million-dollar Mindset is that *you don't need to be a millionaire to have it.* Here are a few things seven-plus-figure business owners have in the forefront of their mind when they evaluate decisions.

THERE ARE THREE TYPES OF LEVERAGE

The most successful and productive people understand that there are three types of leverage you can access to accelerate growth:

1. Leverage of time (hiring someone and delegating).
2. Leverage of money (spending money to solve problems and/or get results faster).
3. Leverage of energy (spending time or money so you don't have to think or act).

Leverage allows you to build momentum without having to use up all your own time and energy. A commitment to utilizing leverage is a huge Mindset shift for entrepreneurs.

Leverage is the way off the hamster wheel so you can scale without killing yourself. More often than not, the best choice is the one that creates the most leverage for you and for your business.

YOUR JOB EACH DAY IS TO MITIGATE RISK

As entrepreneurs, we encounter risk on a daily basis. And even though it isn't fun, and even though at times we try to avoid facing it and dealing with it, it isn't going away anytime soon.

Risk is an inherent part of this human experience (*especially* in business). Given enough time, just about anything and everything can happen. The more risks you handle, deal with, and mitigate, the less fragile your business becomes.

While having good luck is at least partially responsible for a whole bunch of success stories, and unfortunately bad luck is at least partially responsible for most business failures, the truth is that a lot of that bad luck was actually common, foreseeable risk that could have been mitigated but wasn't before it was too late.

Regularly identifying weaknesses, risks, and opportunities, and then *doing something about them* (instead of avoiding them) is the default Mindset and behavior of millionaire entrepreneurs.

When you realize how much risk there is out there, it can be overwhelming. I know what it's like to feel completely powerless in the face of some major risks I've succumbed to as well as just narrowly avoided. The upside here is that when you see the world as high risk, you can take ownership of it. Piece by piece, you can solve for, protect against, and mitigate risks before they have the opportunity to show up (and possibly take you down).

Set a multihour meeting with the key people on your team to brainstorm all the risks you can think of that your business currently faces. Start with the biggest and most likely risks and then work your way down from there. Make it a habit to be regularly solving for the various risks you face.

FEAR OF FAILURE AND SUCCESS

I vividly remember the time I made more money in ONE week than I had the ENTIRE year before, and I had no idea how to process what had just happened. I cried uncontrollably. I called my grandma. I didn't know who else to talk to. I mean, who could help me process experiencing more success than I was used to having in life?

After losing everything and going into over $726,000 of debt, I was able to deal with failure easily enough. But nobody prepared me for how to deal with success. Most people talk about the fear of failure. But who talks about the fear of success? How was I supposed to handle *this*?

That question was very tough for me to answer. Here's why: it comes down to two true Mindset shifts you must understand:

1. Failure is simply a data point that tells us EXACTLY what went wrong. It tells us what didn't go how we expected. It's easy to identify.
2. Success is scarier because most of the time, we're not 100 percent certain how we achieved it, and we aren't fully confident that we can keep creating these elevated results.

This is one of the root causes of the commonly experienced imposter syndrome that entrepreneurs are susceptible to. And I get it. I mean, it is pretty hard to pinpoint the exact thing(s) that created the success(es) we've had so far.

So not only do we not understand HOW what we did made us successful, but we don't know how to handle it. Our minds are conditioned for failure much better than for success. Our DNA has been developed over the years to protect us from ALL elements outside of comfort. That means the discomfort of success can seem like failure, if not worse.

Most of us can imagine huge failure. It's how our brain protects us. We can predict what the worst will look and feel like. Yet when presented with success, especially for the first time, it allows us to access our imagination, creativity, and (for better or worse) our ego and pride in ways we've never imagined.

It's the number one reason that entrepreneurs who find

early success typically lose it all. They don't know how to react to their newfound freedom. Their egos get inflated, and they start to believe they're invincible. As a result, they start making emotionally bad choices.

I know because that happened to me. Both professionally and personally. When I was nineteen, I weighed 360 pounds. And then in sixteen months, I lost 190 pounds. And something strange happened after I lost the weight. Even though my weight was basically cut in half, when I looked in the mirror, I still saw the much larger version of myself.

This happens a lot when you have a huge change in your life, like I did with my weight (and then again years later with handling increased levels of business success). Your mind takes time to catch up with reality.

You want to have checks and balances in place to be able to ground you back to reality (see the Finance Pillar for a lot of that) because of the ability for your mind to not have to believe what the objective reality would lead most people to believe, which means we can create a reality distortion field for ourselves that can help us keep on the path of our goals and our vision even when most other people might think we're crazy for doing so.

LESS CUSTOMERS VS. MORE CUSTOMERS

As demonstrated in the Product Pillar of this guide, there are several powerful reasons to focus on serving a smaller number of clients on a deeper, more intimate level as opposed to selling at lower value points to a larger number of clients or customers. We also saw how starting at the bottom of the value ladder is a trap that will keep you on the hamster wheel for as long as you continue using that strategy, and it's an insidious trap because there is a logic (albeit flawed) to the argument of starting from the bottom. But you don't have to start from (or continue to occupy) the bottom of the value ladder. And obvious Drake jokes aside, it is much better to be here at the top couple levels on the value ladder.

The truth is, when you are providing deep transformation or growth or healing or simply value (monetary or otherwise), there is a path to not just higher profits but, more importantly, a business that provides you with true freedom that likely involves serving fewer clients but on a deeper, more intimate level.

I challenge you to start brainstorming on, researching into, and talking to your clients about the ways you can deliver more value (as well as the offer(s) you can make to be the vehicle delivering that increased value). Also get clear on *who* you most want to serve in this deeper way. Figure out what values (or traits or attitudes) that exist among the people who have been absolutely energizing for you to work with.

And please be aware that you aren't going to completely flip the switch in one day. But you're only going to get where you want to go if you start moving a few degrees closer to your ideal reality, outcome(s), and your felt experience running your business—*now*.

And once you've started, be consistent in regularly aligning and calibrating yourself closer and closer to the ideal. A consistent commitment is ultimately far more important than the speed that you start out moving at.

It's important to remember that it's *always* helpful to have a clear vision of what that *ideal vision* you're moving toward is. The more vivid your vision is, the better you can articulate it both for yourself as well as for how you communicate it to the world. Start there. And make a commitment to revisit your vision at least once a week and to refresh it at least once a year (ideally once a quarter).

Mindset is actually the most important pillar. The two main reasons for that:

1. You can find someone else to own any of the other five Pillars in your business. Not only that, the people in charge of them will likely change over time, but you,

always and forever, will be the only person responsible for your own Mindset.

2. Entrepreneurship is all about managing risk, overcoming obstacles, managing energy, and managing emotions. Difficult things are going to happen (and we can include handling success well as something that is often emotionally difficult). How are you going to handle these things as they come?

It is my belief that the biggest thing hurting businesses is the limited and/or flawed Mindsets of the entrepreneurs that run them.

Even a business that was set up perfectly in each of the other five Pillars would eventually decay, be overtaken by competition, or become sabotaged from the inside if the entrepreneur running it fails to regularly evolve their Mindset over time.

For most entrepreneurs, Mindset is by far one of the most difficult pillars; the reason is that it's based on how our mind works. And our mind works based on the way that it was trained.

Just because we know something, doesn't mean we are going to go with what we know. Rather, our neural pathways have ways that have been learned. It's why we might feel unmotivated. It's why we spend money we don't have. It's why we stay on the hamster wheel.

The subconsciousness leads the conscious mind nearly 95 percent of the day, and thus, the Mindset is the most difficult part to be able to evolve. Unlike other systems, the mind doesn't have an easy system to apply.

It's based on your determination to be able to rewire stories and patterns that have defined your life. Most of the time, it's also based on your creating a new identity, time and time again. A new set of beliefs, and even values, for your ability to get to the next mountain top.

If there's a single thing an entrepreneur must have in order to achieve success, both in the short and long term, it's the ability to have a Mindset that is growth-oriented for that person not to hang on to an old set of beliefs and stories and for the person to allow for new information to change what they believe is law.

Most of us have a hypothesis, theories, and laws. The best entrepreneurs don't keep laws. They change their beliefs with new information, not just because it worked that way always.

Just ask Kodak, or any business that failed on that one. Over all the chapters, if you can't evolve your Mindset, you're screwed. If you've been stuck for a while, it's your Mindset. If you aren't growing, it's your Mindset.

How you do one thing is how you do everything. It's why I

believe that entrepreneurs need to work on their Mindset every day. In my experience, entrepreneurs will always find different modalities to evolve the mind, and my belief is that everyone has a different set of tools that will work.

Doing things like reading, therapy, hypnotherapy, and other things that get us out of our heads so we can work on our mind; however, what works for me, might not for you.

One thing is for certain with entrepreneurship and your Mindset: your beliefs will change quickly and your mind will evolve quickly. That is, if you want to grow your business. What served you once, won't now.

In this section, I wanted to include a few of the major topics that I encounter with all entrepreneurs that I work with and myself. While I've developed a few programs specifically on Mindset that you can find on my website, this is the overview of them, as each is its own book.

NOT LOVING YOURSELF

I would expect that a lot of entrepreneurs became an entrepreneur because they didn't have a deep love of themselves. You might experience the want to work and work, putting yourself into your work and gaining the outside experience and accolades in order to feel like you can love yourself.

With my therapist a few years ago, he asked me, "Why do you love yourself?"

I listed twenty things. Not a single one had to do with me, as a person. It was all the things I did.

If you want emptiness forever, don't let yourself love yourself. Entrepreneurship can be filled with love, but not if you don't allow yourself to love yourself.

MONEY MINDSET

Most entrepreneurs are broke, and it's not because they don't know how to make money. Most are broke because:

1. They have a hatred of money, or they don't value what it can do. Simply put, they don't really believe that having more of it will make sense. For me, this happened where I thought I would lose anything I had, so I would spend it all.
2. They are afraid of what their family and friends will think and that they will get kicked out of the tribe, which is a mentality that is deep-wired as part of the human experience.
3. They can't simply visualize a life that is easy; they want things to be hard because that's what they know. Simple means that they have to accept that they are somehow chosen and that they can truly have what they want.

This is a lot to fathom. In each case of why someone doesn't have money, the Mindset has to change too.

Profit is good, it will change the world. Further, you must go from being an adolescent with money to being an adult and realizing that, someday, your business might change, the market might change, or you might not have the advantage you have today. Seize the day.

TRUST

If you're reading this book, it's likely that you don't trust yourself the way you should, or aren't scaling the way you should because you don't have a team.

Trust inside of business is important. First, you must trust yourself, which, more than likely, is hard. I mean, we've both done a lot of dumb things. Worse, we've done a lot of smart things that didn't give us what we expected. I didn't think that I'd go a million in debt. I didn't think a lot of the things that went wrong would go wrong. And yet, you and I are here, having to trust ourselves as the creator of our destiny. That can be scary.

Then, if we can get past that, we have to trust others. We have to trust our finance person. We have to trust our accountant. We have to trust our operations person. How can we trust someone else? Is it blind trust? Digging ourselves in a hole?

In my experience, I've adopted a belief of trusting everyone until they give me a reason not to trust them. This isn't about going into things blind. However, I've found that if you trust someone, they will live up to that expectation. People respond to you, the way you treat them.

Trust is the reason so many self-improvement programs make money. And it's the number one reason why entrepreneurs won't get momentum quickly.

BEING SEEN

It was 2016. I just surpassed 50,000 people on my email list. I was freaking out. I had a full-out panic attack. All of these people are listening to me; what do I do now? I mean, am I even qualified enough?

At every stage of entrepreneurship and leveling up, you will battle the Mindset of being seen. No matter if it has to do with how much money you make or how big your audience is. Or how someone will introduce you. It's normal to have an inner guilt or judgment about being seen. That you aren't good enough. That you're an imposter.

Everyone I've ever met and mentored has a glass ceiling, and I guarantee that if you stay there, your gifts won't ever make it to their potential on planet earth.

CONFIDENCE

There's the confidence in your work and results, which, at the beginning, might be difficult. Then there's self-confidence that you can make this work.

Part of entrepreneurship is seeing something before it has come into reality. Each and every day can be a struggle if you don't have confidence.

How can you pitch the big dream to someone if you don't have the results to back it up? And if you have the results to back it up, what if this didn't hit like your last thing?

Every time someone hires me and pays me a LOT of money, I still have this come up. When will I work with someone and it doesn't hit the way I want?

Keeping your confidence and the inner game behind that is one of the most difficult things you'll ever deal with. You get so many messages in society, and you get so much comparison of others in social media, how can someone even look in the mirror and say, "I've got this"?

EGO

Ego is the sharpest double-edged sword I've ever found. Through it, you can create enough delusion to accomplish anything. And through it, you can fall and not even realize it.

Ego, however, isn't the enemy. It's what the world-self can do to you if you let it.

See, your ego has a very important job. It allows you to wake up each morning and say, "You've got this. You can beat the odds."

Without ego, most entrepreneurs would crumble on the first day. They wouldn't even start.

Yet, if you have an unhealthy relationship with your ego, you will get stuck in a reality distortion field, unable to see your blind spots and unable to see the world the way it actually is. Each and every day, you must check it with a healthy dose of reality and humility and then get back to work on the development of yourself.

IDENTITY

The issue with being an entrepreneur and even what I teach in this book is not having a stuck identity.

For years, I was the marketing guy. Then I was the guy to help you scale a seven-plus-figure business. Now, I'm the guy who helps influencers and the best in the world build online businesses.

In each version of who you are in the world, both online

and offline, there's a version of what people will see you as and then the version of who you are.

Your persona, no matter how authentic, will always be different than you because you will evolve faster. You will change your mind. You will surpass the version that someone created of you.

Yet, you feel a little weird with this. "If I post X, or launch Y, what will people think?"

It's one of the reasons people stay in their lane too long, which results in burnout, fatigue, and lack of passion, all the death words of an entrepreneur.

FAILURE AND SUCCESS

Failure is easier to understand than success. Most people are afraid of success. They are afraid of who they actually are. They are afraid of what success will actually create in their life. Thus, I see so many people sabotage their success so they can stay with what they know, which is failure.

Failure is easy. We want to avoid it, but just enough of it.

Success is scary—it's the reason that this book took so long to write and publish. Because I'm afraid of it blowing up. I'm afraid of the success I knew that I was capable of.

This book has been dedicated to giving you the Six Pillars of what will unleash The Nuclear Effect; however, Mindset is the most important.

At every level in your business, you will experience new sensations and new opportunities. New things to cry about and things that will truly make you question if you want to continue.

Mindset and developing is the glue that will allow you to continue to expand and grow. I've found that anytime my Mindset has become stuck, my business has as well. If I was ready to quit, I forgot why I was in business, or my ego was running the business.

For you, from my heart, all I can give you as the action with Mindset is this: it will all be okay. Keep building, keep learning, keep loving, and don't take life too seriously. It's all a game, even if it doesn't feel like that today.

SO HOW DOES THE NUCLEAR EFFECT HELP YOU?

You probably dedicated the time, thought, and energy. On follow-through, you bought this book for the same reasons why I wrote it.

If there was even just *one* thing in the previous pages that better equips you to turn your innate vision into reality or helps you experience greater freedom in life or helps put together a puzzle piece or two for you as you figure out how the heck to make this whole business thing more successful, my suggestion is that you *leverage* it to the fullest.

Make the most of your opportunities in the lifetime of each opportunity. And if you see the same potential that I do for the kind of impact The Nuclear Effect can make on your business, make a commitment to leveraging the whole system to its fullest. Because when you do, you will begin to see just how much (and how relatively quickly) The Nuclear Effect can amplify the levels of success, freedom, abundance, and impact you experience.

My belief is that, as entrepreneurs, we have extreme power over our business and over our life. However, it requires us to step up and take a level of responsibility, and this book is mostly about that. Taking your head out of the sand and using methods, frameworks, and concepts that are proven— that may or may not be fun or exciting. But here's the truth, my friend: entrepreneurship is fun, but running a business isn't always.

A billionaire once said to me, "My fortune was built on the back of repetition, not on the back of innovation."

As entrepreneurs, we are natural quick-starts, innovators, disrupters, and rebels. I wrote this book for you so that you could build your business and then either hire someone to run it, pivot it, or sell it.

The worse thing an entrepreneur can do is to start something and then not allow that value to get out into the world. Further, your net worth will come down to the number of people you help and at the extent of that value.

Most entrepreneurs are broke, not because they don't have great ideas or haven't built great companies; it's because they got bored and quit. This book is about growing your business as quickly as possible. If it's a little boring, that's okay. You don't have to run THIS business, forever.

However, if you give it a little time and follow this advice, you'll have a business that thrusts you into an entirely new place in your life.

Now that you are armed with this knowledge, I am *even more* excited to see just how much success and impact you can create moving forward. In truth, I want for you:

- The ability to build an audience so you can leverage your brand.
- The ability for you to generate revenue and profit so you can change your life and the life of those around you.
- The ability for you to build relationships so you have opportunities that you don't have today.

That is what The Nuclear Effect is all about.

CAN I CONTINUE HELPING YOU AS YOU MOVE FORWARD FROM HERE?

While I shared *a lot* in this book about The Nuclear Effect and how to activate it through key improvements to each of your Six Pillars, there are some things that are *very difficult* to help people change, transform, or upgrade through static text in a book.

At first, I wrote about our entire line of products, where we can help. However, more than anything, I know that I can help you. So I'll make this short and sweet.

I wrote this book to help the entrepreneur before me. Today, my purpose is to help other entrepreneurs evolve more quickly. Thus, if you're ready, I'd love to see if I can help you.

Visit here: ScottOldford.com. I'd love to see where you are in your business, and from there, I can tell you exactly how I can help. I'm excited to serve you. I'm excited to help you.

And if you enjoyed this and want to get into the next level, I've prepared a special masterclass for you. There's a couple hoops to jump through, but I promise, it'll give you the next level in all of this.

CONCLUSION

If you've made it here, you've just experienced the critical elements of what it takes to take your online business to the next level. Not the fluff, nor the "one quick thing," but rather, the real things that entrepreneurs have to work on.

In my time, I've helped hundreds of entrepreneurs who've been scaling past seven figures, and when they implement this, they find a massive shift occurs in their business.

However, it's important to realize that the Six Pillars of your business continually move and flow as you evolve. It's an exercise that you need to do weekly, or monthly at the minimum. When you know where you are going and you have clarity, you're able to get there much faster.

Throughout this book, I've shared models and frameworks

that have been tested time and time again because building a business is a pattern-based process. While building a business might seem like pulling a lot of strings and hoping to see which ones work, it's far more predictable than you might expect. However, because you haven't done it the way that makes sense, it seems complex, a little scary and potentially like one big roller coaster.

Most Entrepreneurs are never able to scale their business successfully. The reason is because they don't take the pillars seriously. You can have an amazing mindset and finances, but without marketing and sales, you will grow so slowly that the opportunity in the market will disappear. Your marketing and sales might be the best in the world; however, if you can't deliver and operate the business, your reputation will get hurt, and no amount of marketing will be able to save you. You might have a business scaling extremely well; however, if your mindset doesn't scale with it, you will sabotage yourself into being broke, again.

In everything I've given you inside this book, I can tell you with certainty that building a business isn't easy. If so, everyone would have successful, profitable businesses. It's about being able to continue to build yourself and your team, along with ensuring you maintain and grow each pillar faster and sooner than you might want to.

In life, everything that can break, will break. That's the

point of business. To solve problems. In solving those problems, you will create new ones. No matter where you are with your business today. Regardless if it's burning down, busting at the seams, or ticking along nicely.

On every edge of growth and scale, the longer you don't implement what you need to into each, the slower you will grow, or the faster you will implode.

For you, I want the best, because when you have a successful business, life seems to go much smoother. And when your own life is better, you can do so much more for this world—it needs all the help it can get.

In essence and conclusion, *The Nuclear Effect* is the combination of all Six Pillars working together. Marketing and Sales working together to be able to turn complete strangers into those who REALLY want your help. Operations, Finance and Delivery working together so that you can scale the value you deliver so that you can turn a profit and so that you have a culture that you're proud of (and so you can take a vacation at some point). And Mindset, the glue that holds everything together, so you just don't throw up your hands when there's a fire and say, "That's it!"

The Nuclear Effect doesn't just create a successful and sustainable business that produces profit. Because, as I've spoken about with you, it produces audience, influence, and relationships that you would never have otherwise.

I believe that in the future, money is going to be useful. But not as useful. You will be able to generate wealth from relationships, audience, and influence far more quickly than from money itself.

And your business, when inside of The Nuclear Effect, can create all forms of currency while developing each and everyday assets in the form of a business that can be sold or, at the least, influence an audience that can be utilized for new businesses, opportunities, and the ability to serve in a greater way.

The Nuclear Effect, since its finding, has generated hundreds of millions of dollars for those who have activated it, while building influence, audience, and relationships and allowing for once no-name Entrepreneurs to become their category king and queens.

I truly believe that we are all entrepreneurs; it's embedded in our blood. Most of the time, struggle, and hustle is paralleled with entrepreneurship. For good reason.

I simply hope that with this book and what you've been able to learn from me now and in the future, that it can be easier. Through the power of information, action, mentorship, coaching, and accountability, you can turn the difficult into the possibility of a lifetime.

Now, it's your chance to take it. Ready to dive into more? This is just the beginning.

Visit: ScottOldford.com.

ACKNOWLEDGMENTS

I believe that as human beings, we are typically a reflection of our environment.

As entrepreneurs, this is amplified even more because we are attempting to accomplish what seems like the impossible.

These pages contain everything I've learned that I could bring into a singular book, and it's built upon years of research, practice, and implementation. However, after spending over a million dollars in coaching, mentorship, and consuming others' strategies and frameworks, all of what I know is because of those that came before me.

Entrepreneurship is by far one of the most exciting experiences you can ever have, however, you could never do it without the people that stand beside you each and every day. My parents and grandparents from the start, allowing me to have these amazing experiences and allowing me to get up when I fell down (often), along with my wife, Libby Crow, who continues to be my biggest supporter and the reason why this book even happened, knowing that it HAD to be released into the world, no ifs, ands, or buts.

For every person that has helped me in any way. Every mentor, coach, entrepreneur, every person's book I've ever read, conference, or mastermind I've attended. Thank you, truly. I wouldn't be anywhere without you, I deeply love all of you.

ABOUT THE AUTHOR

SCOTT OLDFORD's strategies and tactics for scaling online businesses has been viewed by millions of people and has directly helped hundreds of 6 and 7+ figure businesses to scale up.

For over twenty years, he's worked in various niches, industries, and business models, and now specializes as an investor and advisor to entrepreneurs and influencers who are positively impacting the world with their work.

While *The Nuclear Effect* is only one framework that he uses inside of helping other businesses, his work has been featured in *Entrepreneur, Inc., Business Insider, Time, Forbes,* and countless other publications.

Those who work with him are typically attracted by the

business strategy and tactic while having a level of being grounded in the mindset and mentality needed for success—not just being successful in business but in all elements of life.

Scott lives in Northern California with his wife, Libby Crow (a fellow entrepreneur and influencer) and their miniature wiener dog—Cooper.

Scott believes that by helping entrepreneurs—some of the most powerful and influential people on the planet—he will be able to evolve the consciousness of the planet, and the easiest way to do that is ensure that entrepreneurs can scale a business with ease and flow instead of difficulty and hustle.